Phonics and Word Recognition

Grade **K**

TABLE OF CONTENTS

About *Benchmark Advance* Intervention

Benchmark Advance Intervention is intended for students who need extra support to master grade-level standards. It offers reteaching and additional practice to reinforce instruction in the core program. *Benchmark Advance* Intervention provides direct instruction of the Reading Standards for Foundational Skills, Grades K–5, as outlined in the Common Core State Standards. The standards are addressed as shown below.

Kindergarten	Grade 1	Grade 2	Grade 3	Grades 4–6
Print Concepts	Print Concepts	Print Concepts	Print Concepts	Phonics and Word Recognition
Phonological Awareness	Phonological Awareness	Phonological Awareness	Phonological Awareness	Fluency
Phonics and Word Recognition	Phonics and Word Recognition	Phonics and Word Recognition	Phonics and Word Recognition	
Fluency	Fluency	Fluency	Fluency	

At Grades K–3, individual grade-level packages of lessons and blackline masters address all of the Reading Foundation (RF) standards. An additional package for Grades 4–6 addresses the Phonics and Word Recognition and Fluency standards for Grades 2–5. In addition, each of the packages at Grades K–3 includes lessons and blackline masters to address the RF standards presented in previous grades. In this way, teachers can address the needs of students at each student's instructional level—whether at/near grade level or below.

The program offers skill-focused sequential and systematic instruction that is parallel to instruction in the core program. Each lesson is designed to target a specific skill that needs bolstering as revealed through program assessments.

It can be implemented flexibly in small groups or to individual students. Each lesson is designed to be completed in 15 minutes.

Lesson Structure

All of the phonics and word recognition lessons in *Benchmark Advance* Intervention follow a consistent instructional design that offers explicit skills instruction and a gradual release model to scaffold student learning.

The side column at the start of every lesson furnishes the information teachers need to manage student learning:

- The target CCSS standard or standards

- The specific lesson objective that states what students will be able to do after completing the lesson

- The metacognitive strategy that students will use as they learn

- The essential academic language and materials that students will use in the lesson are listed

- A reminder of the prerequisite skills that students need to fully understand the lesson

The instructional lessons offer consistent and explicit instruction that helps students focus on the specific lesson objectives:

- The Introduce and State Learning Goal sections set the learning goal for the lesson.

- The Teach and Model sections of the lesson feature direct instruction and teacher modeling, including phonemic awareness and sound/ spelling correspondence.

- The Practice and Apply sections offer guided and independent practice of the focus skill including practice reading high-frequency words and decodable text, and writing spelling words.

- The Conclusion gives students an opportunity to restate what they've learned in the lesson.

- The Home Connection sidebar links the lesson to at-home practice within the family setting.

Every lesson ends with a point-of-use formative assessment so teachers can evaluate whether students have mastered the target skills. Intervention 2 suggestions provide alternative teaching ideas for working with students who need further support.

The blackline masters that accompany the lessons provide practice and application opportunities to promote standards mastery.

Corrective Feedback

Inherent in the teaching profession is the need to make corrections. In both structural and communicative approaches to language teaching and learning, feedback is viewed as a means of fostering learner motivation and ensuring linguistic accuracy (Ellis 2009). The purpose of the feedback is to close the gap between the student's current learning status and the lesson goals (Sadler, 1989). Students can receive feedback in three ways: from their teachers, from peers, and through self-assessment.

Formative assessment is a process that teachers and students use during instruction. It provides feedback to inform ongoing teaching and learning approaches. Corrective feedback is also an essential feature of language development instruction. Teachers provide students with judiciously selected corrective feedback on language usage in ways that are transparent and meaningful to students. Overcorrection or arbitrary corrective feedback is avoided.

Corrective feedback is information given to learners regarding a linguistic error they have made (Loewen 2012; Sheen 2007). The feedback information can consist of any one or all of the following:

(a) **an indication that an error has been committed,**

(b) **provision of the correct target language form, or**

(c) **metalinguistic information about the nature of the error.**

Corrective feedback in the form of negotiating for meaning can help learners notice their errors and create meaningful connections, thus aiding acquisition. It is important to emphasize that language learners can only self-correct if they possess the necessary linguistic knowledge (Ellis 2003).

One solution sometimes advocated to this problem is to conduct corrective feedback as a two-stage process: first encourage self-correction and then, if that fails, provide the correction (Doughty and Varela, 1998).

Corrective feedback can be:

Explicit
Explicit corrective feedback overtly draws the learner's attention to the error made.

Implicit
Implicit corrective feedback focuses the learner's attention without overtly informing the learner that he/she has made an error or interrupting the flow of interaction.

Corrective Feedback Strategies

	IMPLICIT Attracts learner's attention without overtly informing the learner that he/she has made an error or interrupting the flow of interaction.	EXPLICIT Tries to overtly draw the learner's attention to the error made.
INPUT PROVIDING: **Correct form is given to students.**	**RECAST** The teacher incorporates the content words of the immediately preceding incorrect utterance and changes and corrects the utterance in some way (e.g., phonological, syntactic, morphological, or lexical). L: I went school. T: You went to school?	**EXPLICIT CORRECTION** The teacher indicates an error has been committed, identifies the error, and provides the correction. L: We will go on May. T: Not *on* May, *in* May. T: We will go in May.
OUTPUT PROMPTING: **The student is prompted to self-correct.**	**REPETITION** The teacher repeats the learner utterance highlighting the error by means of emphatic stress. L: I will showed you. T: I will *show* you. L: I will show you.	**METALINGUISTIC EXPLANATION** Teacher provides explanation for the errors that have been made. L: two duck T: Do you remember how to show more than one duck? L: ducks T: Yes, you remember that we need to add "s" at the end of a noun to show the plural form.
	CLARIFICATION REQUEST The teacher indicates that he/she has not understood what the learner said. L: on the it go T: Can you please tell me again? T: Do you mean "it goes on your desk"?	**ELICITATION** The teacher repeats part of the learner utterance but not the erroneous part and uses rising intonation to signal the learner should complete it. L: I don't think won't rain. T: I don't think it …(will) rain.
		PARALINGUISTIC SIGNAL The teacher uses a gesture or facial expression to indicate that the learner has made an error. L: Yesterday I go to the movies. T: (gestures with right forefinger over left shoulder to indicate past)

Adapted from: Ellis, Rod. "Corrective Feedback and Teacher Development," L2 Journal, Volume 1 (2009).

Recommendations for English Learners

Student Language and Literacy Characteristics	Considerations for Instructions
Oral Skills — No or little spoken English proficiency	**Students will need instruction in recognizing and distinguishing the sounds of English as compared or contrasted with sounds in their native language.** • Use visuals and gestures to convey that in English, letters are symbols that represent sounds and that words are a sequence of letters that make up a word that conveys meaning.

Oral skills: Spoken English proficiency	**Students will need instruction in applying their knowledge of the English sound system to foundational literacy learning.**
	• Take an inventory of students, oral vocabulary. Draw upon students' known and familiar oral vocabulary to
	  • Clap syllables in known words.
	  • Segment and blend syllables of known words.
	  • Listen to the sequence of sounds in known words.
	  • Use visuals to support comprehension.

Print Skills — No or little native language literacy	**Students will need instruction in print concepts.**
	• As students develop an understanding of the organization and basic features of print, they learn that spoken words in English are composed of smaller elements of speech and that letters represent these sounds (alphabetical principle).
	• Instruction systematically includes
	  1. Following words from left to right, top to bottom, and page by page.
	  2. Recognizing that spoken words are represented in written language by specific sequences of letters.
	  3. Understanding that words are separated by spaces in print.
	  4. Recognizing and naming all upper- and lowercase letters of the alphabet.
	  5. Recognizing the distinguishing features of a sentence (e.g., first word, capitalization, ending punctuation).

Some foundational literacy proficiency in a language not using the Latin alphabet (e.g., Arabic, Chinese, Korean, Russian)	**Students will be familiar with print concepts, and will need instruction in learning the Latin alphabet for English, as compared or contrasted with their native language writing system (e.g., direction of print, symbols representing whole words, syllables or phonemes).**
	• For students who have been taught to use a logographic system, an introduction to the alphabet is necessary and the instruction needs to include sound-symbol relationships (Chinese languages, Korean).
	• For students who use an alphabetic language that does not use the Latin alphabet, an introduction to the alphabet is necessary and the instruction needs to include sound-symbol relationships (Greek, Arabic, Russian).
	  • Compare and contrast directionality and print orientation:
	  • Left to right, top to bottom: Greek, Russian, Brahmic, Thai
	  • Right-to-left orientation, top to bottom: Arabic, Hebrew, Persian, Syriac, Urdu

Some foundational literacy proficiency in a language using the Latin alphabet (e.g., Spanish)	**Students will need instruction in applying their knowledge of print concepts, phonics and word recognition to the English writing system, as compared or contrasted with their native language alphabet (e.g., letters that are the same or different, or represent the same or different sounds) and native language vocabulary (e.g., cognates) and sentence structure (e.g., subject-verb-object vs. subject-object-verb word order).** • Most languages that use the Latin alphabet have the same line direction (left to right) and same block direction (top to bottom). (English, Spanish, French, Portuguese)

Please see the Contrastive Analysis Charts provided in the Teacher's Resource System.

Identify and Name Initial Consonant Mm RF.K.3a, RF.K.3c

CCSS: RF.K.3
Know and apply grade-level phonics and word analysis skills in decoding words both in isolation and in text..
a. Demonstrate basic knowledge of one-to-one letter-sound correspondences by producing the primary sound or many of the most frequent sounds for each consonant.
c. Read common high-frequency words by sight.

Lesson Objectives

- Identify and name the letter **Mm**.
- Produce the sound of letter **Mm**.
- Relate the sound /**m**/ to the letter **Mm**.
- Recognize initial sound /**m**/ in words/pictures.
- Read common high-frequency words: **I**.

Metacognitive Strategy
- Selective Auditory Attention

Academic Language
- letter name, letter sound, initial sound, high-frequency word

Additional Materials
- Sound Spelling Card **Mm**
- Poetry Poster "Melons and Muffins"
- Blackline Masters 1, 2

Pre-Assess
Student's ability to recognize the sound represented by the targeted letter of the alphabet and to identify the letter used to represent the corresponding sound.

Introduce

As students participate in this lesson, they will identify the name and sound of the targeted letter and will identify the letter when the sound and name is given orally. They will apply their knowledge by recognizing the initial sound of the target letter using pictures. They will also apply the skill in context by reading decodable simple sentences that include high-frequency words.

State Learning Goal

Say: Today we will practice matching the sound and letter **m**.

Display Sound Spelling Card Mm.

Say: This is capital **M**. This is lowercase **m**.

Teach

Say: Letters represent sounds. We remember the sounds each letter makes. We use letters to write words we say. We use letters to read and write words.

Shared Reading

Use the poetry poster "Melons and Muffins." Read the poem aloud emphasizing rhythm and rhyme,, and target sound. Invite students to echo-read or chime in the rhyme on cue.

Phonemic Awareness

Show the picture of the sound/spelling card to review the sound.

Say: This is the **Mm** card. Listen to this sound /**m**/. Say it with me: /**m**/. Now say it on your own: /**m**/.

Display the poetry poster and read it aloud.

Sound-Spelling Correspondence

Show the letter.

Say: The way we write the sound /**m**/ is with the letter **m**. The letter **m** makes the sound /**m**/.

Ask: What is the name of the letter? (**m**) What sound does the letter make? /**m**/

Model

Use BLM 1, Row 1.

Say: We will look at each picture. Say its name. If we hear the sound /**m**/ at the beginning of the word, we will circle the picture. If we do not hear the sound /**m**/ at the beginning, we will cross out the picture.

Ask: What do you see in the first picture? (**mitt**) Do you hear the sound /**m**/ at the beginning of the word **mitt**?

Say: Circle the letter **m**. If you do not hear the sound /**m**/ at the beginning of the word, then cross out the picture. Repeat with other words.

Practice

Use BLM 1, Row 2.

Say: *Look at the picture. Say its name. Write the letter.*

Ask: *What do you see in the second picture?* (**mat**) *Do you hear the sound /**m**/ at the beginning of the word* **mat**? *Write the letter* **m**. Repeat with other words.

Apply
Blend Words

Use BLM 1, Row 3

Say: *Look at each letter and listen to the sound as I read:* /**m**/ /**a**/ /**n**/. *Your turn:* /**m**/ /**a**/ /**n**/.

Say: *Now we are going to blend the sounds together by stretching them out as we read them.* Point to each letter in a sweeping motion left to right /**mmmaaannn**/.

Ask: *What is the word?* (**man**) Repeat with other words.

High-Frequency words

Use BLM 1, Row 4.

Say: *First, I will point to the word and read it. Then, you will point to the word and we will read it together. Next, I will read a word and you will point to it. Now, you will read the word and I will point to it. Let's write/trace the word as we spell it:* **I.**

Decodable Text

Use BLM 2, Row 1.

Say: *First, I will point to each word as I read the sentence. Then, you will point to each word and we will read together. Next, I will read the sentence and you will point to each word as I read. Now, you will point to each word as you read. Circle all the examples of the letter* **m** *you find in this sentence. Circle the word* **I** *in the sentences.*

Spelling

Use BLM 2, Row 2.

Say: *Now we can practice writing the sounds we hear in each word. Say one word at a time, stretching each sound. Write a letter for each sound you hear.*

Conclusion

Ask: *What did we learn today? What pictures/words will help you remember the sound /**m**/ and the letter* **m**?

Say: *We learned that the letter* **m** *makes the sound /**m**/. We wrote words using the letter* **m**.

Home Connection

Ask students to practice identifying initial sound /**m**/ and writing the letter **m** with a family member. Have students identify other words that begin with letter **m** with their family.

✔ Formative Assessment

If the student completes each task correctly, proceed to the next skill in the sequence. If not, refer to suggested Intervention 2.

Did the student…?	Intervention 2
Identify the names of the letters?	• Use physical rhythmic movements as the letter name is repeated. March while chanting the letter name. Move arms up and down. Sway from side to side.
Identify the sounds of the letters?	• Use alliteration, chants that repeat the sound several times, then a word that begins with the sound. Example: /**m**/ /**m**/ /**m**/ mat.
Produce the sounds of the letters?	• Use mirrors to show the movement of the mouth, tongue, and teeth as the sound is produced. Use hand over mouth to explore movement of air as the sound is produced.
Recognize the beginning sounds?	• Use Elkonin boxes – student moves a token into the first box as the beginning sound of the word is said.
Write the letters?	• Write the letter; have students trace it. Create the letter with clay. • Discuss the letter features (lines, shape). Trace over the letter with multiple colors.
Know the names of the pictures?	• Tell students the name of the pictures; have students repeat them aloud. • Discuss the words and use each word in context.
Read high-frequency words?	• Create take-home word cards. Use a reward system to track words learned over time. The student uses the word in a sentence, and the teacher writes it down and highlights the high-frequency word. The student re-reads it the next day.

Identify and Name Initial Consonant Ss RF.K.3a, RF.K.3c

CCSS: RF.K.3
Know and apply grade-level phonics and word analysis skills in decoding words both in isolation and in text.
a. Demonstrate basic knowledge of one-to-one letter-sound correspondences by producing the primary sound or many of the most frequent sounds for each consonant.
c. Read common high-frequency words by sight.

Lesson Objectives

- Identify and name the letter **Ss.**
- Produce the sound of letter **Ss.**
- Relate the sound **/s/** to the letter **Ss.**
- Recognize initial sound **/s/** in words/pictures.
- Read common high-frequency words: **the, we.**

Metacognitive Strategy
- Selective Auditory Attention

Academic Language
- letter name, letter sound, initial sound, high-frequency word

Additional Materials
- Sound Spelling Card **Ss**
- Poetry Poster "Seven Silly Sailors"
- Blackline Masters 3, 4

Pre-Assess
Student's ability to recognize the sound represented by the targeted letter of the alphabet and to identify the letter used to represent the corresponding sound.

Introduce

As students participate in this lesson, they will identify the name and sound of the targeted letter, and will identify the letter when the sound and name is given orally. They will apply their knowledge by recognizing the initial sound of the target letter using pictures. They will also apply the skill in context by reading decodable simple sentences that include high-frequency words.

State Learning Goal

Say: Today we will practice matching the sound and letter **s**.

Display Sound Spelling Card **Ss**.

Say: This is capital **S**. This is lowercase **s**.

Teach

Say: Letters represent sounds. We remember the sounds each letter makes. We use letters to write words we say. We use letters to read and write words.

Shared Reading

Use the poetry poster "Seven Silly Sailors." Read the poem aloud emphasizing rhythm and rhyme,, and target sound. Invite students to echo-read or chime in the rhyme on cue.

Phonemic Awareness

Show the picture of the sound/spelling card to review the sound.

Say: This is the **s** card. Listen to this sound /**s**/. Say it with me: **s.** Now say it on your own: **s**.

Display the poetry poster and read it aloud again.

Sound-Spelling Correspondence

Show the letter.

Say: The way we write the sound /**s**/ is with the letter **s**. The letter **s** makes the sound /**s**/.

Ask: What is the name of the letter? (**S**) What sound does the letter make? /**s**/.

Model

Use BLM 3, Row 1.

Say: We will look at each picture. Say its name. If we hear the sound /**s**/ at the beginning of the word, we will circle the picture. If we do not hear the sound /**s**/ at the beginning, we will cross out the picture.

Ask: What do you see in the first picture? (**sit**) Do you hear the sound /**s**/ at the beginning of the word **sit**?

Say: Circle the letter **s**. If you do not hear the sound /**s**/ at the beginning of the word, then cross out the picture. Repeat with other words.

Practice

Use BLM 3, Row 2.

Say: *Look at the picture. Say its name. Write the letter.*

Ask: *What do you see in the second picture?* (**son**). *Do you hear the sound* **/s/** *at the beginning of the word son? Write the letter* **s**. *Repeat with other words.*

Apply

Blend Words

Use BLM 3, Row 3

Say: *Look at each letter and listen to the sound as I read:* **/S/ /a/ /m/**. *Your turn:* **/S/ /a/ /m/**. *Now we are going to blend the sounds together by stretching them out as we read them.* Point to each letter in a sweeping motion left to right **/sssaaammm/**.

Ask: *What is the word?* (**Sam**) *Repeat with other words.*

High-Frequency words

Use BLM 3, Row 4.

Say: *First, I will point to the word and read it. Then, you will point to the word and we will read it together. Next, I will read a word and you will point to it. Now, you will read the word and I will point to it. Let's write/trace the word as we spell it:* **the**.

Decodable Text

Use BLM 4, Row 1.

Say: *First, I will point to each word as I read the sentence. Then, you will point to each word and we will read together. Next, I will read the sentence and you will point to each word as I read. Now, you will point to each word as you read. Circle all the examples of the letter* **s** *you find in this sentence. Circle the words* **we** *and* **the** *in the sentences.*

Spelling

Use BLM 4, Row 2.

Say: *Now we can practice writing the sounds we hear in each word. Say one word at a time, stretching each sound. Write a letter for each sound you hear.*

Conclusion

Ask: *What did we learn today? What pictures/words will help you remember the sound* **/s/** *and the letter* **s**?

Say: *We learned that the letter* **s** *makes the sound* **/s/**. *We wrote words using the letter* **s**.

Home Connection

Ask students to practice identifying initial sound **/s/** and writing the letter **s** with a family member. Have students identify other words that begin with letter **s** with their family.

✔ Formative Assessment

If the student completes each task correctly, proceed to the next skill in the sequence. If not, refer to suggested Intervention 2.

Did the student…?	Intervention 2
Identify the names of the letters?	• Use physical rhythmic movements as the letter name is repeated. March while chanting the letter name. Move arms up and down. Sway from side to side.
Identify the sounds of the letters?	• Use alliteration, chants that repeat the sound several times, then a word that begins with the sound. Example: /s/ /s/ /s/ **sap**.
Produce the sounds of the letters?	• Use mirrors to show the movement of the mouth, tongue, and teeth as the sound is produced. Use hand over mouth to explore movement of air as the sound is produced.
Recognize the beginning sounds?	• Use Elkonin boxes – student moves a token into the first box as the beginning sound of the word is said.
Write the letters?	• Write the letter; have students trace it. Create the letter with clay. • Discuss the letter features (lines, shape). Trace over the letter with multiple colors.
Know the names of the pictures?	• Tell students the name of the pictures; have students repeat them aloud. • Discuss the words and use each word in context.
Read high-frequency words?	• Create take-home word cards. Use a reward system to track words learned over time. The student uses the word in a sentence, and the teacher writes it down and highlights the high-frequency word. The student re-reads it the next day.

Identify and Name Initial Consonant Tt RF.K.3a, RF.K.3c

CCSS:RF.K.3
Know and apply grade-level phonics and word analysis skills in decoding words both in isolation and in text.
a. Demonstrate basic knowledge of one-to-one letter-sound correspondences by producing the primary sound or many of the most frequent sounds for each consonant.
c. Read common high-frequency words by sight.

Lesson Objectives

- Identify and name the letter **Tt**.
- Produce the sound of letter **Tt**.
- Relate the sound /**t**/ to the letter **Tt**.
- Recognize initial sound /**t**/ in words/pictures.
- Read common high-frequency words: **see**, **go**.

Metacognitive Strategy
- Selective Auditory Attention

Academic Language
- letter name, letter sound, initial sound, high-frequency word

Additional Materials
- Sound Spelling Card **Tt**
- Poetry Poster "Turtles"
- Blackline Masters 5, 6

Pre-Assess
Student's ability to recognize the sound represented by the targeted letter of the alphabet and to identify the letter used to represent the corresponding sound.

Introduce

As students participate in this lesson, they will identify the name and sound of the targeted letter and will identify the letter when the sound and name is given orally. They will apply their knowledge by recognizing the initial sound of the target letter using pictures. They will also apply the skill in context by reading decodable simple sentences that include high-frequency words.

State Learning Goal
Say: *Today we will practice matching the sound and letter* **t**

Display Sound Spelling Card **Tt**.

Say: *This is capital* **T**. *This is lowercase* **t**

Teach

Say: *Letters represent sounds. We remember the sounds each letter makes. We use letters to write words we say. We use letters to read and write words.*

Shared Reading
Use the poetry poster "Turtles." Read the poem aloud emphasizing rhythm and rhyme,, and target sound. Invite students to echo-read or chime in the rhyme on cue.

Phonemic Awareness
Show the picture of the sound/spelling card to review the sound.

Say: *This is the* **Tt** *card. Listen to this sound* /**t**/. *Say it with me:* **t**. *Now say it on your own:* **t**

Display the poetry poster and read it aloud.

Sound-Spelling Correspondence
Show the letter.

Say: *The way we write the sound* /**t**/ *is with the letter* **t**. *The letter* **t** *makes the sound* /**t**/.

Ask: *What is the name of the letter?* (**t**) *What sound does the letter make?* /**t**/.

Model
Use BLM 5, Row 1.

Say: *We will look at each picture. Say its name. If we hear the sound* /**t**/ *at the beginning of the word, we will circle the picture. If we do not hear the sound* /**t**/ *at the beginning, we will cross out the picture.*

Ask: *What do you see in the first picture?* (**tip**) *Do you hear the sound* /**t**/ *at the beginning of the word* **tip**?

Say: *Circle the letter* **t** *If you do not hear the sound* /**t**/ *at the beginning of the word, then cross out the picture.* **Repeat with other words.**

Practice

Use BLM 5, Row 2.

Say: *Look at the picture. Say its name. Write the letter.*

Ask: *What do you see in the second picture?* (**tan**) *Do you hear the sound /**t**/ at the beginning of the word* **tan**? *Write the letter* **t**. *Repeat with other words.*

Apply

Blend Words

Use BLM 5, Row 3.

Say: *Look at each letter and listen to the sound as I read: /**t**/ /**o**/ /**p**/. Your turn: /**t**/ /**o**/ /**p**/.*

Say: *Now we are going to blend the sounds together by stretching them out as we read them.* Point to each letter in a sweeping motion left to right /**tooop**/.

Ask: *What is the word?* (**top**) *Repeat with other words.*

High-Frequency words

Use BLM 5, Row 4.

Say: *First, I will point to the word and read it. Then, you will point to the word and we will read it together. Next, I will read a word and you will point to it. Now, you will read the word and I will point to it. Let's write/trace the word as we spell it:* **see**.

Decodable Text

Use BLM 6, Row 1.

Say: *First, I will point to each word as I read the sentence. Then, you will point to each word and we will read together. Next, I will read the sentence and you will point to each word as I read. Now, you will point to each word as you read. Circle all the examples of the letter* **t** *you find in this sentence. Circle the words* **see** *and* **go** *in the sentences.*

Spelling

Use BLM 6, Row 2.

Say: *Now we can practice writing the sounds we hear in each word. Say one word at a time, stretching each sound. Write a letter for each sound you hear.*

Conclusion

Ask: *What did we learn today? What pictures/words will help you remember the sound /**t**/ and the letter* **t**?

Say: *We learned that the letter* **t** *makes the sound /**t**/. We wrote words using the letter* **t**.

Home Connection

Ask students to practice identifying initial sound /**t**/ and writing the letter **t** with a family member. Have students identify other words that begin with letter **t** with their family.

✔ Formative Assessment

If the student completes each task correctly, proceed to the next skill in the sequence. If not, refer to suggested Intervention 2.

Did the student…?	Intervention 2
Identify the names of the letters?	• Use physical rhythmic movements as the letter name is repeated. March while chanting the letter name. Move arms up and down. Sway from side to side..
Identify the sounds of the letters?	• Use alliteration, chants that repeat the sound several times, then a word that begins with the sound. Example: /**t**/ /**t**/ /**t**/ tan.
Produce the sounds of the letters?	• Use mirrors to show the movement of the mouth, tongue, and teeth as the sound is produced. • Use hand over mouth to explore movement of air as the sound is produced.
Recognize the beginning sounds?	• Use Elkonin boxes – student moves a token into the first box as the beginning sound of the word is said.
Write the letters?	• Write the letter; have students trace it. Create the letter with clay. • Discuss the letter features (lines, shape). Trace over the letter with multiple colors.
Know the names of the pictures?	• Tell students the name of the pictures; have students repeat them aloud. • Discuss the words and use each word in context.
Read high-frequency words?	• Create take-home word cards. Use a reward system to track words learned over time. The student uses the word in a sentence, and the teacher writes it down and highlights the high-frequency word. The student re-reads it the next day.

Identify and Name Initial Consonant Nn RF.K.3a, RF.K.3c

CCSS: RF.K.3
Know and apply grade-level phonics and word analysis skills in decoding words both in isolation and in text.
a. Demonstrate basic knowledge of one-to-one letter-sound correspondences by producing the primary sound or many of the most frequent sounds for each consonant.
c. Read common high-frequency words by sight.

Lesson Objectives

- Identify and name the letter **Nn**.
- Produce the sound of letter **Nn**.
- Relate the sound /**n**/ to the letter **Nn**.
- Recognize initial sound /**n**/ in words/pictures.
- Read common high-frequency words: **I, like, the, see.**

Metacognitive Strategy
- Selective Auditory Attention

Academic Language
- letter name, letter sound, initial sound, high-frequency word

Additional Materials
- Sound Spelling Card **Nn**
- Poetry Poster "Nip the Newt"
- Blackline Masters 7, 8

Pre-Assess
Student's ability to recognize the sound represented by the targeted letter of the alphabet and to identify the letter used to represent the corresponding sound.

Introduce

As students participate in this lesson, they will identify the name and sound of the targeted letter and will identify the letter when the sound and name is given orally. They will apply their knowledge by recognizing the initial sound of the target letter using pictures. They will also apply the skill in context by reading decodable simple sentences that include high-frequency words.

State Learning Goal
Say: *Today we will practice matching the sound and letter* **n**.

Display Sound Spelling Card **Nn**.

Say: *This is capital* **N**. *This is lowercase* **n**.

Teach
Say: *Letters represent sounds. We remember the sounds each letter makes. We use letters to write words we say. We use letters to read and write words.*

Shared Reading
Use the poetry poster "Nip the Newt." Read the poem aloud emphasizing rhythm and rhyme, and target sound. Invite students to echo-read or chime in the rhyme on cue.

Phonemic Awareness
Show the picture of the sound/spelling card to review the sound.

Say: *This is the* **Nn** *card. Listen to this sound* /**n**/. *Say it with me:* **n**. *Now say it on your own:* **n**

Display the poetry poster and read it aloud again.

Sound-Spelling Correspondence
Show the letter **Nn**.

Say: *The way we write the sound* /**n**/ *is with the letter* **n**. *The letter* **n** *makes the sound* /**n**/.

Ask: *What is the name of the letter?* (**n**) *What sound does the letter make?* /**n**/.

Model
Use BLM 7, Row 1.

Say: *We will look at each picture. Say its name. If we hear the sound* /**n**/ *at the beginning of the word, we will circle the picture. If we do not hear the sound* /**n**/ *at the beginning, we will cross out the picture.*

Ask: *What do you see in the first picture?* (**nap**) *Do you hear the sound* /**n**/ *at the beginning of the word nap?*

Say: *Circle the letter* **n**. *If you do not hear the sound* /**n**/ *at the beginning of the word, then cross out the picture.* Repeat with other words.

Practice

Use BLM 7, Row 2.

Say: *Look at the picture. Say its name. Write the letter.*

Ask: *What do you see in the second picture?* (**Nat**) *Do you hear the sound /n/ at the beginning of the word* **Nat**? *Write the letter* **n**. *Repeat with other words.*

Apply

Blend Words

Use BLM 7, Row 3.

Say: *Look at each letter and listen to the sound as I read:* /**n**/ /**o**/ /**t**/. *Your turn:* /**n**/ /**o**/ /**t**/.

Say: *Now we are going to blend the sounds together by stretching them out as we read them.* Point to each letter in a sweeping motion left to right /**nnnooot**/.

Ask: *What is the word?* (**not**) *Repeat with other words.*

High-Frequency words

Use BLM 7, Row 4.

Say: *First, I will point to the word and read it. Then, you will point to the word and we will read it together. Next, I will read a word and you will point to it. Now, you will read the word and I will point to it. Let's write/trace the word as we spell it:* **I**.

Decodable Text

Use BLM 8, Row 1.

Say: *First, I will point to each word as I read the sentence. Then, you will point to each word and we will read together. Next, I will read the sentence and you will point to each word as I read. Now, you will point to each word as you read. Circle all the examples of the letter* **n** *you find in this sentence. Circle the words* **I**, **like**, **see**, *and* **the** *in the sentences.*

Spelling

Use BLM 8, Row 2.

Say: *Now we can practice writing the sounds we hear in each word. Say one word at a time, stretching each sound. Write a letter for each sound you hear.*

Conclusion

Ask: *What did we learn today? What pictures/words will help you remember the sound /n/ and the letter* **n**?

Say: *We learned that the letter* **n** *makes the sound /n/. We wrote words using the letter* **n**.

Home Connection

Ask students to practice identifying initial sound /**n**/ and writing the letter **n** with a family member. Have students identify other words that begin with letter **n** with their family.

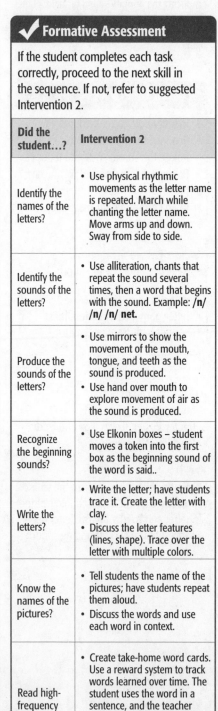

✔ Formative Assessment

If the student completes each task correctly, proceed to the next skill in the sequence. If not, refer to suggested Intervention 2.

Did the student…?	Intervention 2
Identify the names of the letters?	• Use physical rhythmic movements as the letter name is repeated. March while chanting the letter name. Move arms up and down. Sway from side to side.
Identify the sounds of the letters?	• Use alliteration, chants that repeat the sound several times, then a word that begins with the sound. Example: /**n**/ /**n**/ /**n**/ net.
Produce the sounds of the letters?	• Use mirrors to show the movement of the mouth, tongue, and teeth as the sound is produced. • Use hand over mouth to explore movement of air as the sound is produced.
Recognize the beginning sounds?	• Use Elkonin boxes – student moves a token into the first box as the beginning sound of the word is said..
Write the letters?	• Write the letter; have students trace it. Create the letter with clay. • Discuss the letter features (lines, shape). Trace over the letter with multiple colors.
Know the names of the pictures?	• Tell students the name of the pictures; have students repeat them aloud. • Discuss the words and use each word in context.
Read high-frequency words?	• Create take-home word cards. Use a reward system to track words learned over time. The student uses the word in a sentence, and the teacher writes it down and highlights the high-frequency word. The student re-reads it the next day.

Identify and Name Initial Consonant Ff RF.K.3a, RF.K.3c

CCSS: RF.K.3
Know and apply grade-level phonics and word analysis skills in decoding words both in isolation and in text.
a. Demonstrate basic knowledge of one-to-one letter-sound correspondences by producing the primary sound or many of the most frequent sounds for each consonant.
c. Read common high-frequency words by sight.

Lesson Objectives

- Identify and name the letter **Ff**.
- Produce the sound of letter **Ff**.
- Relate the sound /**f**/ to the letter **Ff**.
- Recognize initial sound /**f**/ in words/pictures.
- Read common high-frequency words: **is, a**.

Metacognitive Strategy
- Selective auditory attention

Academic Language
- letter name, letter sound, initial sound, high-frequency word

Additional Materials
- Sound Spelling Card **Ff**
- Poetry Poster "Fuzzy Fox and Fiddle"
- Blackline Masters 9, 10

Pre-Assess
Student's ability to recognize the sound represented by the targeted letter of the alphabet and to identify the letter used to represent the corresponding sound.

Introduce

As students participate in this lesson, they will identify the name and sound of the targeted letter and will identify the letter when the sound and name is given orally. They will apply their knowledge by recognizing the initial sound of the target letter using pictures. They will also apply the skill in context by reading decodable simple sentences that include high-frequency words.

State Learning Goal

Say: *Today we will practice matching the sound and letter* **f**.

Display Sound Spelling Card **Ff**.

Say: *This is capital* **F**. *This is lowercase* **f**.

Teach

Say: *Letters represent sounds. We remember the sounds each letter makes. We use letters to write words we say. We use letters to read and write words.*

Shared Reading

Use the poetry poster "Fuzzy Fox and Fiddle." Read the poem aloud emphasizing rhythm and rhyme, and target sound. Invite students to echo-read or chime in the rhyme on cue.

Phonemic Awareness

Show the picture of the sound/spelling card to review the sound.

Say: *This is the* **Ff** *card. Listen to this sound* /**f**/. *Say it with me:* **f**. *Now say it on your own:* **f**.

Display the poetry poster and read it aloud again.

Sound-Spelling Correspondence

Show the letter.

Say: *The way we write the sound* /**f**/ *is with the letter* **f**. *The letter* **f** *makes the sound* /**f**/.

Ask: *What is the name of the letter?* (**f**) *What sound does the letter make?* /**f**/.

Model

Use BLM 9, Row 1.

Say: *We will look at each picture. Say its name. If we hear the sound* /**f**/ *at the beginning of the word, we will circle the picture. If we do not hear the sound* /**f**/ *at the beginning, we will cross out the picture.*

Ask: *What do you see in the first picture?* (**fan**) *Do you hear the sound* /**f**/ *at the beginning of the word?*

Say: *Circle the picture. If you do not hear the sound* /**f**/ *at the beginning of the word, then cross out the picture.* **Repeat with other words.**

Practice

Use BLM 9, Row 2.

Say: *Look at the picture. Say its name. Write the letter.*

Ask: *What do you see in the first picture?* (**fig**) *Do you hear the sound /f/ at the beginning of the word* **fig**? *Write the letter* **f**. *Repeat with other words.*

Apply
Blend Words

Use BLM 9, Row 3.

Say: *Look at each letter and listen to the sound as I read: /f/ /i/ /n/. Your turn: /f/ /i/ /n/.*

Say: *Now we are going to blend the sounds together by stretching them out as we read them.* Point to each letter in a sweeping motion left to right /**fffiiinnn**/.

Ask: *What is the word?* (**fin**) *Repeat with other words.*

High-Frequency words

Use BLM 9, Row 4.

Say: *First, I will point to the word and read it. Then, you will point to the word and we will read it together. Next, I will read a word and you will point to it. Now, you will read the word and I will point to it. Let's write/trace the word as we spell it:* **is**.

Decodable Text

Use BLM 10, Row 1.

Say: *First, I will point to each word as I read the sentence. Then, you will point to each word and we will read together. Next, I will read the sentence and you will point to each word as I read. Now, you will point to each word as you read. Circle all the examples of the letter* **f** *you find in this sentence. Circle the words* **is** *and* **a** *in the sentences.*

Spelling

Use BLM 10, Row 2.

Say: *Now we can practice writing the sounds we hear in each word. Say one word at a time, stretching each sound. Write a letter for each sound you hear.*

Conclusion

Ask: *What did we learn today? What pictures/words will help you remember the sound /f/ and the letter* **f**?

Say: *We learned that the letter* **f** *makes the sound /f/. We wrote words using the letter* **f** .

Home Connection

Ask students to practice identifying initial sound /**f**/ and writing the letter **f** with a family member. Have students identify other words that begin with letter **f** with their family.

✓ Formative Assessment	
If the student completes each task correctly, proceed to the next skill in the sequence. If not, refer to suggested Intervention 2.	
Did the student…?	**Intervention 2**
Identify the names of the letters?	• Use physical rhythmic movements as the letter name is repeated. March while chanting the letter name. Move arms up and down. Sway from side to side..
Identify the sounds of the letters?	• Use alliteration, chants that repeat the sound several times, then a word that begins with the sound. Example: /**f**/ /**f**/ /**f**/ **fan**.
Produce the sounds of the letters?	• Use mirrors to show the movement of the mouth, tongue, and teeth as the sound is produced. • Use hand over mouth to explore movement of air as the sound is produced.
Recognize the beginning sounds?	• Use Elkonin boxes – student moves a token into the first box as the beginning sound of the word is said. .
Write the letters?	• Write the letter; have students trace it. Create the letter with clay. • Discuss the letter features (lines, shape). Trace over the letter with multiple colors.
Know the names of the pictures?	• Tell students the name of the pictures; have students repeat them aloud. • Discuss the words and use each word in context.
Read high-frequency words?	• Create take-home word cards. Use a reward system to track words learned over time. The student uses the word in a sentence, and the teacher writes it down and highlights the high-frequency word. The student re-reads it the next day.

Identify and Name Initial Consonant Pp RF.K.3a, RF.K.3c

CCSS: RF.K.3
Know and apply grade-level phonics and word analysis skills in decoding words both in isolation and in text.
a. Demonstrate basic knowledge of one-to-one letter-sound correspondences by producing the primary sound or many of the most frequent sounds for each consonant.
c. Read common high-frequency words by sight.

Lesson Objectives

- Identify and name the letter **Pp.**
- Produce the sound of letter **Pp.**
- Relate the sound **/p/** to the letter **Pp.**
- Recognize initial sound **/p/** in words/pictures.
- Read common high-frequency words: **we, see, is, a**

Metacognitive Strategy
- Selective Auditory Attention

Academic Language
- letter name, letter sound, initial sound, high-frequency word

Additional Materials
- Sound Spelling Card **Pp**
- Poetry Poster "Pet Parade"
- Blackline Masters 11, 12

Pre-Assess
Student's ability to recognize the sound represented by the targeted letter of the alphabet and to identify the letter used to represent the corresponding sound.

Introduce

As students participate in this lesson, they will identify the name and sound of the targeted letter and will identify the letter when the sound and name is given orally. They will apply their knowledge by recognizing the initial sound of the target letter using pictures. They will also apply the skill in context by reading decodable simple sentences that include high-frequency words.

State Learning Goal

Say: *Today we will practice matching the sound and letter* **p**.

Display Sound Spelling Card **Pp**.

Say: *This is capital* **P**. *This is lowercase* **p**.

Teach

Say: *Letters represent sounds. We remember the sounds each letter makes. We use letters to write words we say. We use letters to read and write words.*

Shared Reading

Use the poetry poster "Pet Parade." Read the poem aloud emphasizing rhythm and rhyme, and target sound. Invite students to echo-read or chime in the rhyme on cue.

Phonemic Awareness

Show the picture of the sound/spelling card to review the sound. This is the **Pp** card.

Say: *Listen to this sound /*p*/. Say it with me:* **p** *Now say it on your own:* **p**.

Display the poetry poster and read it aloud again.

Sound-Spelling Correspondence

Show the letter.

Say: *The way we write the sound /*p*/ is with the letter* **p**. *The letter* **p** *makes the sound /*p*/.*

Ask: *What is the name of the letter?* (**p**) *What sound does the letter make?* /**p**/.

Model

Use BLM 11, Row 1.

Say: *We will look at each picture. Say its name. If we hear the sound /*p*/ at the beginning of the word, we will circle the picture. If we do not hear the sound /*p*/ at the beginning, we will cross out the picture.*

Ask: *What do you see in the first picture?* (**pan**) *Do you hear the sound /*p*/ at the beginning of the word?*

Say: *Circle the letter* **p**. *If you do not hear the sound /*p*/ at the beginning of the word, then cross out picture.* Repeat with other words.

Practice

Use BLM 11, Row 2.

Say: *Look at the picture. Say its name. Write the letter.*

Ask: *What do you see in the first picture?* (**pin**) *Do you hear the sound /**p**/ at the beginning of the word* **pin**? *Write the letter* **p***. Repeat with other words.*

Apply

Blend Words

Use BLM 11, Row 3.

Say: *Look at each letter and listen to the sound as I read: /**p**/ /**i**/ /**t**/. Your turn: /**p**/ /**i**/ /**t**/.*

Say: *Now we are going to blend the sounds together by stretching them out as we read them.* Point to each letter in a sweeping motion left to right /**piiit**/.

Ask: *What is the word?* (**pit**) *Repeat with other words.*

High-Frequency words

Use BLM 11, Row 4.

Say: *First, I will point to the word and read it. Then, you will point to the word and we will read it together. Next, I will read a word and you will point to it. Now, you will read the word and I will point to it. Let's write/trace the word as we spell it:* **a***.*

Decodable Text

Use BLM 12, Row 1.

Say: *First, I will point to each word as I read the sentence. Then, you will point to each word and we will read together. Next, I will read the sentence and you will point to each word as I read. Now, you will point to each word as you read. Circle the words* **a, is, see,** *and* **we** *in the sentences.*

Spelling

Use BLM 12, Row 2.

Say: *Now we can practice writing the sounds we hear in each word. Say one word at a time, stretching each sound. Write a letter for each sound you hear.*

Conclusion

Ask: *What did we learn today? What pictures/words will help you remember the sound /**p**/ and the letter* **p**?

Say: *We learned that the letter* **p** *makes the sound /**p**/. We wrote words using the letter* **p***.*

Home Connection

Ask students to practice identifying initial sound /**p**/ and writing the letter **p** with a family member. Have students identify other words that begin with letter **p** with their family.

✔ Formative Assessment

If the student completes each task correctly, proceed to the next skill in the sequence. If not, refer to suggested Intervention 2.

Did the student…?	Intervention 2
Identify the names of the letters?	• Use physical rhythmic movements as the letter name is repeated. March while chanting the letter name. Move arms up and down. Sway from side to side.
Identify the sounds of the letters?	• Use alliteration, chants that repeat the sound several times, then a word that begins with the sound. Example: /**p**/ /**p**/ /**p**/ **pan**.
Produce the sounds of the letters?	• Use mirrors to show the movement of the mouth, tongue, and teeth as the sound is produced. • Use hand over mouth to explore movement of air as the sound is produced.
Recognize the beginning sounds?	• Use Elkonin boxes – student moves a token into the first box as the beginning sound of the word is said.
Write the letters?	• Write the letter; have students trace it. Create the letter with clay. • Discuss the letter features (lines, shape). Trace over the letter with multiple colors.
Know the names of the pictures?	• Tell students the name of the pictures; have students repeat them aloud. • Discuss the words and use each word in context.
Read high-frequency words?	• Create take-home word cards. Use a reward system to track words learned over time. The student uses the word in a sentence, and the teacher writes it down and highlights the high-frequency word. The student re-reads it the next day.

Identify and Name Initial Consonant Cc RF.K.3a, RF.K.3c

CCSS: RF.K.3
Know and apply grade-level phonics and word analysis skills in decoding words both in isolation and in text.
a. Demonstrate basic knowledge of one-to-one letter-sound correspondences by producing the primary sound or many of the most frequent sounds for each consonant.
c. Read common high-frequency words by sight.

Lesson Objectives

- Identify and name the letter **Cc.**
- Produce the sound of letter **Cc.**
- Relate the sound **/k/** to the letter **Cc.**
- Recognize initial sound of **/k/** in words/pictures.
- Read common high-frequency words: **little, play**

Metacognitive Strategy
- Selective Auditory Attention

Academic Language
- letter name, letter sound, initial sound, high-frequency word

Additional Materials
- Sound Spelling Card **Cc**
- Poetry Poster "Camping"
- Blackline Masters 13, 14

Pre-Assess
Student's ability to recognize the sound represented by the targeted letter of the alphabet and to identify the letter used to represent the corresponding sound.

Introduce

As students participate in this lesson, they will identify the name and sound of the targeted letter and will identify the letter when the sound and name is given orally. They will apply their knowledge by recognizing the initial sound of the target letter using pictures. They will also apply the skill in context by reading decodable simple sentences that include high-frequency words.

State Learning Goal
Say: *Today we will practice matching the sound and letter* **c**.

Display Sound Spelling **Cc.**

Say: *This is capital* **C**. *This is lowercase* **c**.

Teach

Say: *Letters represent sounds. We remember the sounds each letter makes. We use letters to write words we say. We use letters to read and write words.*

Shared Reading
Use the poetry poster "Camping." Read the poem aloud emphasizing rhythm and rhyme, and target sound. Invite students to echo-read or chime in the rhyme on cue.

Phonemic Awareness
Show the picture of the sound/spelling card to review the sound.

Say: *This is the* **Cc** *card. Listen to this sound* /**k**/. *Say it with me:* **k** *Now say it on your own:* **k**.

Display the poetry poster and read it aloud again.

Sound-Spelling Correspondence
Show the letter.

Say: *The way we write the sound* /**k**/ *is with the letter* **c**. *The letter* **c** *makes the sound* /**k**/.

Ask: *What is the name of the letter?* (**c**) *What sound does the letter make?* /**k**/.

Model
Use BLM 13, Row 1.

Say: *We will look at each picture. Say its name. If we hear the sound* /**k**/ *at the beginning of the word, we will circle the picture. If we do not hear the sound* /**k**/ *at the beginning, we will cross out the picture.*

Ask: *What do you see in the first picture?* (**can**) *Do you hear the sound* /**k**/ *at the beginning of the word?*

Say: *Circle the picture. If you do not hear the sound* /**k**/ *at the beginning of the word, then cross out the picture.* Repeat with other words.

Practice

Use BLM 13, Row 2.

Say: *Look at the picture. Say its name. Write the letter.*

Ask: *What do you see in the first picture?* (a **cap**) *Do you hear the sound* /k/ *at the beginning of the word* **cap**? *Write the letter* **c**. *Repeat with other words.*

Apply

Blend Words

Use BLM 13, Row 3.

Say: *Look at each letter and listen to the sound as I read:* /k/ /a/ /r/. *Your turn:* /k/ /a/ /r/.

Say: *Now we are going to blend the sounds together by stretching them out as we read them.* Point to each letter in a sweeping motion left to right /**kaaarrr**/.

Ask: *What is the word?* (**car**) *Repeat with other words.*

High-Frequency words

Use BLM 13, Row 4.

Say: *First, I will point to the word and read it. Then, you will point to the word and we will read it together. Next, I will read a word and you will point to it. Now, you will read the word and I will point to it. Let's write/trace the word as we spell it:* **little**.

Decodable Text

Use BLM 14, Row 1.

Say: *First, I will point to each word as I read the sentence. Then, you will point to each word and we will read together. Next, I will read the sentence and you will point to each word as I read. Now, you will point to each word as you read. Circle the words* **little** *and* **play** *in the sentences.*

Spelling

Use BLM 14, Row 2.

Say: *Now we can practice writing the sounds we hear in each word. Say one word at a time, stretching each sound. Write a letter for each sound you hear.*

Conclusion

Ask: *What did we learn today? What pictures/words will help you remember the sound* /k/ *and the letter* **c**?

Say: *We learned that the letter* **c** *makes the sound* /k/. *We wrote words using the letter* **c**.

Home Connection

Ask students to practice identifying initial sound /**c**/and writing the letter **c** with a family member. Have students identify other words that begin with letter **c** with their family.

✔ Formative Assessment

If the student completes each task correctly, proceed to the next skill in the sequence. If not, refer to suggested Intervention 2.

Did the student…?	Intervention 2
Identify the names of the letters?	• Use physical rhythmic movements as the letter name is repeated. March while chanting the letter name. Move arms up and down. Sway from side to side.
Identify the sounds of the letters?	• Use alliteration, chants that repeat the sound several times, then a word that begins with the sound. Example: /**k**/ /**k**/ /**k**/ **can**.
Produce the sounds of the letters?	• Use mirrors to show the movement of the mouth, tongue, and teeth as the sound is produced. • Use hand over mouth to explore movement of air as the sound is produced.
Recognize the beginning sounds?	• Use Elkonin boxes – student moves a token into the first box as the beginning sound of the word is said.
Write the letters?	• Write the letter; have students trace it. Create the letter with clay. • Discuss the letter features (lines, shape). Trace over the letter with multiple colors.
Know the names of the pictures?	• Tell students the name of the pictures; have students repeat them aloud. • Discuss the words and use each word in context.
Read high-frequency words?	• Create take-home word cards. Use a reward system to track words learned over time. The student uses the word in a sentence, and the teacher writes it down and highlights the high-frequency word. The student re-reads it the next day.

©2017 Benchmark Education Company, LLC   **BENCHMARK ADVANCE** • Intervention • Phonics and Word Recognition • Grade K   **15**

Identify and Name Initial Consonant Hh RF.K.3a, RF.K.3c

CCSS: RF.K.3
Know and apply grade-level phonics and word analysis skills in decoding words both in isolation and in text..
a. Demonstrate basic knowledge of one-to-one letter-sound correspondences by producing the primary sound or many of the most frequent sounds for each consonant.
c. Read common high-frequency words by sight.

Lesson Objectives

- Identify and name the letter **Hh**.
- Produce the sound of letter **Hh**.
- Relate the sound /**h**/ to the letter **Hh**.
- Recognize initial sound /**h**/ in words/pictures.
- Read common high-frequency words: **a, has, he, little**

Metacognitive Strategy
- Selective Auditory Attention

Academic Language
- letter name, letter sound, initial sound, high-frequency word

Additional Materials
- Sound Spelling Card **Hh**
- Poetry Poster "Happy Thoughts"
- Blackline Masters 15, 16

Pre-Assess
Student's ability to recognize the sound represented by the targeted letter of the alphabet and to identify the letter used to represent the corresponding sound.

Introduce

As students participate in this lesson, they will identify the name and sound of the targeted letter and will identify the letter when the sound and name is given orally. They will apply their knowledge by recognizing the initial sound of the target letter using pictures. They will also apply the skill in context by reading decodable simple sentences that include high-frequency words.

State Learning Goal

Say: Today we will practice matching the sound and letter **h**.

Display Sound Spelling Card **Hh**.

Say: This is capital **H**. This is lowercase **h**.

Teach

Say: Letters represent sounds. We remember the sounds each letter makes. We use letters to write words we say. We use letters to read and write words.

Shared Reading

Use the poetry poster "Happy Thoughts." Read the poem aloud emphasizing rhythm and rhyme, and target sound. Invite students to echo-read or chime in the rhyme on cue.

Phonemic Awareness

Show the picture of the sound/spelling card to review the sound.

Say: This is the **Hh** card. Listen to this sound /**h**/. Say it with me: **h**. Now say it on your own: **h**.

Display the poetry poster and read it aloud again.

Sound-Spelling Correspondence

Show the letter.

Say: The way we write the sound /**h**/ is with the letter **h**. The letter **h** makes the sound /**h**/.

Ask: What is the name of the letter? (**h**) What sound does the letter make? /**h**/.

Model

Use BLM 15, Row 1.

Say: We will look at each picture. Say its name. If we hear the sound /**h**/ at the beginning of the word, we will circle the picture. If we do not hear the sound /**h**/ at the beginning, we will cross out the picture.

Ask: What do you see in the first picture? (**hat**) Do you hear the sound /**h**/ at the beginning of the word **h**?

Say: Circle the picture. If you do not hear the sound /**h**/ at the beginning of the word, then cross out the picture. Repeat with other words.

Practice

Use BLM 15, Row 2.

Say: *Look at the picture. Say its name. Write the letter.*

Ask: *What do you see in the first picture?* (**horse**) *Do you hear the sound /**h**/ at the beginning of the word* **horse**? *Write the letter* **h**. Repeat with other words.

Apply

Blend Words

Use BLM 15, Row 3.

Say: *Look at each letter and listen to the sound as I read: /**h**/ /**ay**/. Your turn: /**h**/ /**ay**/. Now we are going to blend the sounds together by stretching them out as we read them.* Point to each letter in a sweeping motion left to right /**hay**/. **Ask:** *What word?* (**hay**) Repeat with other words.

High-Frequency words

Use BLM 15, Row 4.

Say: *First, I will point to the word and read it. Then, you will point to the word and we will read it together. Next, I will read a word and you will point to it. Now, you will read the word and I will point to it. Let's write/trace the word as we spell it:* **a**.

Decodable Text

Use BLM 16, Row 1.

Say: *First, I will point to each word as I read the sentence. Then, you will point to each word and we will read together. Next, I will read the sentence and you will point to each word as I read. Now, you will point to each word as you read. Circle all the examples of the letter* **h** *you find in this sentence. Circle the words* **a**, **has**, **he**, *and* **little** *in the sentences.*

Spelling

Use BLM 16, Row 2.

Say: *Now we can practice writing the sounds we hear in each word. Say one word at a time, stretching each sound. Write a letter for each sound you hear.*

Conclusion

Ask: *What did we learn today? What pictures/words will help you remember the sound /**h**/ and the letter* **h**?

Say: *We learned that the letter* **h** *makes the sound /**h**/. We wrote words using the letter* **h**.

Home Connection

Ask students to practice identifying initial sound /**h**/ and writing the letter **h** with a family member. Have students identify other words that begin with letter **h** with their family.

✔ Formative Assessment

If the student completes each task correctly, proceed to the next skill in the sequence. If not, refer to suggested Intervention 2.

Did the student…?	Intervention 2
Identify the names of the letters?	• Use physical rhythmic movements as the letter name is repeated. March while chanting the letter name. Move arms up and down. Sway from side to side.
Identify the sounds of the letters?	• Use alliteration, chants that repeat the sound several times, then a word that begins with the sound. Example: /**h**/ /**h**/ /**h**/ **hat**.
Produce the sounds of the letters?	• Use mirrors to show the movement of the mouth, tongue, and teeth as the sound is produced. • Use hand over mouth to explore movement of air as the sound is produced.
Recognize the beginning sounds?	• Use Elkonin boxes – student moves a token into the first box as the beginning sound of the word is said.
Write the letters?	• Write the letter; have students trace it. Create the letter with clay. • Discuss the letter features (lines, shape). Trace over the letter with multiple colors.
Know the names of the pictures?	• Tell students the name of the pictures; have students repeat them aloud. • Discuss the words and use each word in context.
Read high-frequency words?	• Create take-home word cards. Use a reward system to track words learned over time. The student uses the word in a sentence, and the teacher writes it down and highlights the high-frequency word. The student re-reads it the next day.

Identify and Name Initial Consonant Bb RF.K.3a, RF.K.3c

CCSS: RF.K.3
Know and apply grade-level phonics and word analysis skills in decoding words both in isolation and in text.
a. Demonstrate basic knowledge of one-to-one letter-sound correspondences by producing the primary sound or many of the most frequent sounds for each consonant.
c. Read common high-frequency words by sight.

Lesson Objectives

- Identify and name the letter **Bb**.
- Produce the sound of letter **Bb**.
- Relate the sound /**b**/ to the letter **Bb**.
- Recognize initial sound /**b**/ in words/pictures.
- Read common high-frequency words: **and, you**.

Metacognitive Strategy
- Selective Auditory Attention

Academic Language
- letter name, letter sound, initial sound, high-frequency word

Additional Materials
- Sound Spelling Card **Bb**
- Poetry Poster "Baby Bird"
- Blackline Masters 17, 18

Pre-Assess
Student's ability to recognize the sound represented by the targeted letter of the alphabet and to identify the letter used to represent the corresponding sound.

Introduce

As students participate in this lesson, they will identify the name and sound of the targeted letter and will identify the letter when the sound and name is given orally. They will apply their knowledge by recognizing the initial sound of the target letter using pictures. They will also apply the skill in context by reading decodable simple sentences that include high-frequency words.

State Learning Goal

Say: Today we will practice matching the sound and letter **b**.

Display Sound Spelling Card **Bb**.

Say: This is capital **B**. This is lowercase **b**.

Teach

Say: Letters represent sounds. We remember the sounds each letter makes. We use letters to write words we say. We use letters to read and write words.

Shared Reading

Use the poetry poster "Baby Bird." Read the poem aloud emphasizing rhythm and rhyme, and target sound. Invite students to echo-read or chime in the rhyme on cue.

Phonemic Awareness

Show the picture of the sound/spelling card to review the sound. This is the Bb card.

Say: Listen to this sound /**b**/. Say it with me: /**b**/. Now say it on your own: /**b**/.

Display the poetry poster and read it aloud again.

Sound-Spelling Correspondence

Show the letter.

Say: The way we write the sound /**b**/ is with the letter **b**. The letter **b** makes the sound /**b**/. What is the name of the letter? (**b**) What sound does the letter make? /**b**/.

Model

Use BLM 17, Row 1.

Say: We will look at each picture. Say its name. If we hear the sound /**b**/ at the beginning of the word, we will circle the picture. If we do not hear the sound /**b**/ at the beginning, we will cross out the picture.

Ask: What do you see in the first picture? (**bat**) Do you hear the sound /**b**/ at the beginning of the word?

Say: Circle the picture. If you do not hear the sound /**b**/ at the beginning of the word, then cross out the picture. Repeat with other words.

Practice

Use BLM 17, Row 2.

Say: *Look at the picture. Say its name. Write the letter.*

Ask: *What do you see in the first picture? (a* **bag**). *Do you hear the sound /***b***/ at the beginning of the word* **bag**? *Write the letter* **b**. Repeat with other words.

Apply
Blend Words

Use BLM 17, Row 3.

Say: *Look at each letter and listen to the sound as I read: /***b***/ /***i***/ /***b***/. Your turn: /***b***/ /***i***/ /***b***/.*

Say: *Now we are going to blend the sounds together by stretching them out as we read them.* Point to each letter in a sweeping motion left to right /**biiib**/.

Ask: *What is the word?* (**bib**) Repeat with other words.

High-Frequency words

Use BLM 17, Row 4.

Say: *First, I will point to the word and read it. Then, you will point to the word and we will read it together. Next, I will read a word and you will point to it. Now, you will read the word and I will point to it. Let's write/trace the word as we spell it:* **and**.

Decodable Text

Use BLM 18, Row 1.

Say: *First, I will point to each word as I read the sentence. Then, you will point to each word and we will read together. Next, I will read the sentence and you will point to each word as I read. Now, you will point to each word as you read. Circle all the examples of the letter* **b** *you find in these sentences. Circle the words* **and** *and* **you** *in the sentences.*

Spelling

Use BLM 18, Row 2.

Say: *Now we can practice writing the sounds we hear in each word. Say one word at a time, stretching each sound. Write a letter for each sound you hear.*

Conclusion

Ask: *What did we learn today? What pictures/words will help you remember the sound /***b***/ and the letter* **b**?

Say: *We learned that the letter* **b** *makes the sound /***b***/. We wrote words using the letter* **b**.

Home Connection

Ask students to practice identifying initial sound /**b**/ and writing the letter **b** with a family member. Have students identify other words that begin with letter **b** with their family.

✔ Formative Assessment

If the student completes each task correctly, proceed to the next skill in the sequence. If not, refer to suggested Intervention 2.

Did the student…?	Intervention 2
Identify the names of the letters?	• Use physical rhythmic movements as the letter name is repeated. March while chanting the letter name. Move arms up and down. Sway from side to side.
Identify the sounds of the letters?	• Use alliteration, chants that repeat the sound several times, then a word that begins with the sound. Example: /**b**/ /**b**/ /**b**/ **bat**.
Produce the sounds of the letters?	• Use mirrors to show the movement of the mouth, tongue, and teeth as the sound is produced. • Use hand over mouth to explore movement of air as the sound is produced.
Recognize the beginning sounds?	• Use Elkonin boxes – student moves a token into the first box as the beginning sound of the word is said.
Write the letters?	• Write the letter; have students trace it. Create the letter with clay. • Discuss the letter features (lines, shape). Trace over the letter with multiple colors.
Know the names of the pictures?	• Tell students the name of the pictures; have students repeat them aloud. • Discuss the words and use each word in context.
Read high-frequency words?	• Create take-home word cards. Use a reward system to track words learned over time. The student uses the word in a sentence, and the teacher writes it down and highlights the high-frequency word. The student re-reads it the next day.

Identify and Name Initial Consonant Rr RF.K.3a, RF.K.3c

CCSS: RF.K.3
Know and apply grade-level phonics and word analysis skills in decoding words both in isolation and in text.
a. Demonstrate basic knowledge of one-to-one letter-sound correspondences by producing the primary sound or many of the most frequent sounds for each consonant.
c. Read common high-frequency words by sight.

Lesson Objectives

- Identify and name the letter **Rr.**
- Produce the sound of letter **Rr.**
- Relate the sound /**r**/ to the letter **Rr.**
- Recognize initial sound /**r**/ in words/pictures.
- Read common high-frequency words: **he, you, with, big.**

Metacognitive Strategy
- Selective Auditory Attention

Academic Language
- letter name, letter sound, initial sound, high-frequency word

Additional Materials
- Sound Spelling Card **Rr**
- Poetry Poster "The Race"
- Blackline Masters 19, 20

Pre-Assess
Student's ability to recognize the sound represented by the targeted letter of the alphabet and to identify the letter used to represent the corresponding sound.

Introduce

As students participate in this lesson, they will identify the name and sound of the targeted letter and will identify the letter when the sound and name is given orally. They will apply their knowledge by recognizing the initial sound of the target letter using pictures. They will also apply the skill in context by reading decodable simple sentences that include high-frequency words.

State Learning Goal
Say: *Today we will practice matching the sound and letter* **r**.

Display Sound Spelling Card **Rr**.

Say: *This is capital* **R**. *This is lowercase* **r**.

Teach
Say: *Letters represent sounds. We remember the sounds each letter makes. We use letters to write words we say. We use letters to read and write words.*

Shared Reading
Use the poetry poster "The Race." Read the poem aloud emphasizing rhythm and rhyme, and target sound. Invite students to echo-read or chime in the rhyme on cue.

Phonemic Awareness
Show the picture of the sound/spelling card to review the sound.

Say: *This is the* **Rr** *card. Listen to this sound* /**r**/. *Say it with me:* /**r**/ *Now say it on your own:* /**r**/. *Display the poetry poster and read it aloud.*

Sound-Spelling Correspondence
Show the letter.

Say: *The way we write the sound* /**r**/ *is with the letter* **r**. *The letter* **r** *makes the sound* /**r**/.

Ask: *What is the name of the letter?* (**r**) *What sound does the letter make?* /**r**/

Model
Use BLM 19, Row 1.

Say: *We will look at each picture. Say its name. If we hear the sound* /**r**/ *at the beginning of the word, we will circle the picture. If we do not hear the sound* /**r**/ *at the beginning, we will cross out the picture.*

Ask: *What do you see in the first picture?* (**rat**) *Do you hear the sound* /**r**/ *at the beginning of the word* **rat**?

Say: *Circle the letter* **r**. *If you do not hear the sound* /**r**/ *at the beginning of the word, then cross out the picture.* Repeat with other words.

Practice

Use BLM 19, Row 2.

Say: *Look at the picture. Say its name. Write the letter.*

Ask: *What do you see in the second picture?* (**rip**) *Do you hear the sound /r/ at the beginning of the word* **rip**? *Write the letter* **r**. Repeat with other words.

Apply

Blend Words

Use BLM 19, Row 3.

Say: *Look at each letter and listen to the sound as I read: /r/ /u/ /n/. Your turn: /r/ /u/ /n/. Now we are going to blend the sounds together by stretching them out as we read them.* Point to each letter in a sweeping motion left to right **/rrruuunnn/**.

Ask: *What is the word?* (**run**) Repeat with other words.

High-Frequency words

Use BLM 19, Row 4.

Say: *First, I will point to the word and read it. Then, you will point to the word and we will read it together. Next, I will read a word and you will point to it. Now, you will read the word and I will point to it. Let's write/trace the word as we spell it:* **he**.

Decodable Text

Use BLM 20, Row 1.

Say: *First, I will point to each word as I read the sentence. Then, you will point to each word and we will read together. Next, I will read the sentence and you will point to each word as I read. Now, you will point to each word as you read.* Circle all the examples of the letter **r** you find in these sentences. Circle the words **he, big, you,** and **with** in the sentences.

Spelling

Use BLM 20, Row 2.

Say: *Now we can practice writing the sounds we hear in each word. Say one word at a time, stretching each sound. Write a letter for each sound you hear.*

Conclusion

Ask: *What did we learn today? What pictures/words will help you remember the sound /r/ and the letter* **r**?

Say: *We learned that the letter* **r** *makes the sound /r/. We wrote words using the letter* **r**.

Home Connection

Ask students to practice identifying initial sound /r/ and writing the letter **r** with a family member. Have students identify other words that begin with letter **r** with their family.

✔ Formative Assessment

If the student completes each task correctly, proceed to the next skill in the sequence. If not, refer to suggested Intervention 2.

Did the student...?	Intervention 2
Identify the names of the letters?	• Use physical rhythmic movements as the letter name is repeated. March while chanting the letter name. Move arms up and down. Sway from side to side.
Identify the sounds of the letters?	• Use alliteration, chants that repeat the sound several times, then a word that begins with the sound. Example: /r/ /r/ /r/ **rat**.
Produce the sounds of the letters?	• Use mirrors to show the movement of the mouth, tongue, and teeth as the sound is produced. • Use hand over mouth to explore movement of air as the sound is produced.
Recognize the beginning sounds?	• Use Elkonin boxes – student moves a token into the first box as the beginning sound of the word is said.
Write the letters?	• Write the letter; have students trace it. Create the letter with clay. • Discuss the letter features (lines, shape). Trace over the letter with multiple colors.
Know the names of the pictures?	• Tell students the name of the pictures; have students repeat them aloud. • Discuss the words and use each word in context.
Read high-frequency words?	• Create take-home word cards. Use a reward system to track words learned over time. The student uses the word in a sentence, and the teacher writes it down and highlights the high-frequency word. The student re-reads it the next day.

Identify and Name Initial Consonant Gg RF.K.3a, RF.K.3c

CCSS: RF.K.3
Know and apply grade-level phonics and word analysis skills in decoding words both in isolation and in text.
a. Demonstrate basic knowledge of one-to-one letter-sound correspondences by producing the primary sound or many of the most frequent sounds for each consonant.
c. Read common high-frequency words by sight.

Lesson Objectives

- Identify and name the letter **Gg**.
- Produce the sound of letter **Gg**.
- Relate the sound /**g**/ to the letter **Gg**.
- Recognize initial sound /**g**/ in words/pictures.
- Read common high-frequency words: **jump, one.**

Metacognitive Strategy
- Selective Auditory Attention

Academic Language
- letter name, letter sound, initial sound, high-frequency word

Additional Materials
- Sound Spelling Card **Gg**
- Poetry Poster "By the Garden Gate"
- Blackline Masters 21, 22

Pre-Assess
Student's ability to recognize the sound represented by the targeted letter of the alphabet and to identify the letter used to represent the corresponding sound.

Introduce

As students participate in this lesson, they will identify the name and sound of the targeted letter and will identify the letter when the sound and name is given orally. They will apply their knowledge by recognizing the initial sound of the target letter using pictures. They will also apply the skill in context by reading decodable simple sentences that include high-frequency words.

State Learning Goal

Say: *Today we will practice matching the sound and letter* **g**.

Display Sound Spelling Card **Gg**.

Say: *This is capital* **G**. *This is lowercase* **g**.

Teach

Say: *Letters represent sounds. We remember the sounds each letter makes. We use letters to write words we say. We use letters to read and write words.*

Shared Reading

Use the poetry poster "By the Garden Gate." Read the poem aloud emphasizing rhythm and rhyme, and target sound. Invite students to echo-read or chime in the rhyme on cue.

Phonemic Awareness

Show the picture of the sound/spelling card to review the sound.

Say: *This is the* **Gg** *card. Listen to this sound* /**g**/. *Say it with me:* /**g**/ *Now say it on your own:* /**g**/.

Display the poetry poster and read it aloud.

Sound-Spelling Correspondence

Show the letter.

Say: *The way we write the sound* /**g**/ *is with the letter* **g**. *The letter* **g** *makes the sound* /**g**/.

Ask: *What is the name of the letter?* (**g**) *What sound does the letter make?* /**g**/.

Model

Use BLM 21, Row 1.

Say: *We will look at each picture. Say its name. If we hear the sound* /**g**/ *at the beginning of the word, we will circle the picture. If we do not hear the sound* /**g**/ *at the beginning, we will cross out the picture.*

Ask: *What do you see in the first picture?* (**gull**) *Do you hear the sound* /**g**/ *at the beginning of the word* **gull**?

Say: *Circle the letter* **g**. *If you do not hear the sound* /**g**/ *at the beginning of the word, then cross out the picture.* Repeat with other words.

Practice

Use BLM 21, Row 2.

Say: *Look at the picture. Say its name. Write the letter.*

Ask: *What do you see in the second picture? (**gap**) Do you hear the sound /**g**/ at the beginning of the word **gap**? Write the letter **g**. Repeat with other words.*

Apply

Blend Words

Use BLM 21, Row 3.

Say: *Look at each letter and listen to the sound as I read: /**g**/ /**a**/ /**s**/. Your turn: /**g**/ /**a**/ /**s**/.*

Say: *Now we are going to blend the sounds together by stretching them out as we read them. Point to each letter in a sweeping motion left to right /**gaaasss**/.*

Ask: *What is the word? (**gas**) Repeat with other words.*

High-Frequency words

Use BLM 21, Row 4.

Say: *First, I will point to the word and read it. Then, you will point to the word and we will read it together. Next, I will read a word and you will point to it. Now, you will read the word and I will point to it. Let's write/trace the word as we spell it:* **jump**.

Decodable Text

Use BLM 22, Row 1.

Say: *First, I will point to each word as I read the sentence. Then, you will point to each word and we will read together. Next, I will read the sentence and you will point to each word as I read. Now, you will point to each word as you read. Circle all the examples of the letter **g** you find in these sentences. Circle the words **jump** and **one** in these sentences.*

Spelling

Use BLM 22 Row 2.

Say: *Now we can practice writing the sounds we hear in each word. Say one word at a time, stretching each sound. Write a letter for each sound you hear.*

Conclusion

Ask: *What did we learn today? What pictures/words will help you remember the sound /**g**/ and the letter **g**?*

Say: *We learned that the letter **g** makes the sound /**g**/. We wrote words using the letter **g**.*

Home Connection

Ask students to practice identifying initial sound /**g**/and writing the letter **g** with a family member. Have students identify other words that begin with letter **g** with their family.

✔ Formative Assessment

If the student completes each task correctly, proceed to the next skill in the sequence. If not, refer to suggested Intervention 2.

Did the student…?	Intervention 2
Identify the names of the letters?	• Use physical rhythmic movements as the letter name is repeated. March while chanting the letter name. Move arms up and down. Sway from side to side.
Identify the sounds of the letters?	• Use alliteration, chants that repeat the sound several times, then a word that begins with the sound. Example: /**g**/ /**g**/ /**g**/ **gum**.
Produce the sounds of the letters?	• Use mirrors to show the movement of the mouth, tongue, and teeth as the sound is produced. • Use hand over mouth to explore movement of air as the sound is produced.
Recognize the beginning sounds?	• Use Elkonin boxes – student moves a token into the first box as the beginning sound of the word is said.
Write the letters?	• Write the letter; have students trace it. Create the letter with clay. • Discuss the letter features (lines, shape). Trace over the letter with multiple colors.
Know the names of the pictures?	• Tell students the name of the pictures; have students repeat them aloud. • Discuss the words and use each word in context.
Read high-frequency words?	• Create take-home word cards. Use a reward system to track words learned over time. The The student uses the word in a sentence, and the teacher writes it down and highlights the high-frequency word. The student re-reads it the next day.

Identify and Name Initial Consonant Dd RF.K.3a, RF.K.3c

CCSS: RF.K.3
Know and apply grade-level phonics and word analysis skills in decoding words both in isolation and in text.
a. Demonstrate basic knowledge of one-to-one letter-sound correspondences by producing the primary sound or many of the most frequent sounds for each consonant.
c. Read common high-frequency words by sight.

Lesson Objectives

- Identify and name the letter **Dd.**
- Produce the sound of letter **Dd.**
- Relate the sound /**d**/ to the letter **Dd.**
- Recognize initial sound /**d**/ in words/pictures.
- Read common high-frequency words: **and, you, with, for.**

Metacognitive Strategy
- Selective Auditory Attention

Academic Language
- letter name, letter sound, initial sound, high-frequency word

Additional Materials
- Sound Spelling Card **Dd**
- Poetry Poster "Dot"
- Blackline Masters 23, 24

Pre-Assess
Student's ability to recognize the sound represented by the targeted letter of the alphabet and to identify the letter used to represent the corresponding sound.

Introduce

As students participate in this lesson, they will identify the name and sound of the targeted letter and will identify the letter when the sound and name is given orally. They will apply their knowledge by recognizing the initial sound of the target letter using pictures. They will also apply the skill in context by reading decodable simple sentences that include high-frequency words.

State Learning Goal

Say: Today we will practice matching the sound and letter **d**.

Display Sound Spelling Card **Dd**.

Say: This is capital **D**. This is lowercase **d**.

Teach

Say: Letters represent sounds. We remember the sounds each letter makes. We use letters to write words we say. We use letters to read and write words.

Shared Reading

Use the poetry poster "Dot." Read the poem aloud emphasizing rhythm and rhyme, and target sound. Invite students to echo-read or chime in the rhyme on cue.

Phonemic Awareness

Show picture of sound/spelling card to review the sound.

Say: This is the **Dd** card. Listen to this sound /**d**/. Say it with me: /**d**/ Now say it on your own: /**d**/. Display the poetry poster and read it aloud.

Sound-Spelling Correspondence

Show the letter.

Say: The way we write the sound /**d**/ is with the letter **d**. The letter **d** makes the sound /**d**/.

Ask: What is the name of the letter? (**d**) What sound does the letter make? /**d**/.

Model

Use BLM 23, Row 1.

Say: We will look at each picture. Say its name. If we hear the sound /**d**/ at the beginning of the word, we will circle the picture. If we do not hear the sound /**d**/ at the beginning, we will cross out the picture.

Ask: What do you see in the first picture? (**dog**) Do you hear the sound /**d**/ at the beginning of the word **dog**?

Say: Circle the letter **d**. If you do not hear the /**d**/ sound at the beginning of the word, then cross out the picture. Repeat with other words.

Practice

Use BLM 23, Row 2.

Say: *Look at the picture. Say its name. Write the letter.*

Ask: *What do you see in the second picture?* (**dot**) *Do you hear the sound* /**d**/ *at the beginning of the word* **dot***? Write the letter* **d***.* Repeat with other words.

Apply
Blend Words

Use BLM 23, Row 3.

Say: *Look at each letter and listen to the sound as I read:* /**d**/ /**i**/ /**g**/*. Your turn:* /**d**/ /**i**/ /**g**/*.*

Say: *Now we are going to blend the sounds together by stretching them out as we read them.* Point to each letter in a sweeping motion left to right /**diiig**/*.*

Ask: *What is the word?* (**dig**) Repeat with other words.

High-Frequency words

Use BLM 23, Row 4.

Say: *First, I will point to the word and read it. Then, you will point to the word and we will read it together. Next, I will read a word and you will point to it. Now, you will read the word and I will point to it. Let's write/trace the word as we spell it:* **and***.*

Decodable Text

Use BLM 24, Row 1.

Say: *First, I will point to each word as I read the sentence. Then, you will point to each word and we will read together. Next, I will read the sentence and you will point to each word as I read. Now, you will point to each word as you read. Circle all the examples of the letter* **d** *you find in these sentences. Circle the words* **and, you, with** *and* **for** *in these sentences.*

Spelling

Use BLM 24 Row 2.

Say: *Now we can practice writing the sounds we hear in each word. Say one word at a time, stretching each sound. Write a letter for each sound you hear.*

Conclusion

Ask: *What did we learn today? What pictures/words will help you remember the sound* /**d**/ *and the letter* **d***?*

Say: *We learned that the letter* **d** *makes the sound* /**d**/*. We wrote words using the letter* **d***.*

Home Connection

Ask students to practice identifying initial sound /**d**/ and writing the letter **d** with a family member. Have students identify other words that begin with letter **d** with their family.

✔ Formative Assessment

If the student completes each task correctly, proceed to the next skill in the sequence. If not, refer to suggested Intervention 2.

Did the student...?	Intervention 2
Identify the names of the letters?	• Use physical rhythmic movements as the letter name is repeated. March while chanting the letter name. Move arms up and down. Sway from side to side.
Identify the sounds of the letters?	• Use alliteration, chants that repeat the sound several times, then a word that begins with the sound. Example: /**d**/ /**d**/ /**d**/ **dog**.
Produce the sounds of the letters?	• Use mirrors to show the movement of the mouth, tongue, and teeth as the sound is produced. • Use hand over mouth to explore movement of air as the sound is produced.
Recognize the beginning sounds?	• Use Elkonin boxes – student moves a token into the first box as the beginning sound of the word is said.
Write the letters?	• Write the letter; have students trace it. Create the letter with clay. • Discuss the letter features (lines, shape). Trace over the letter with multiple colors.
Know the names of the pictures?	• Tell students the name of the pictures; have students repeat them aloud. • Discuss the words and use each word in context.
Read high-frequency words?	• Create take-home word cards. Use a reward system to track words learned over time. The student uses the word in a sentence, and the teacher writes it down and highlights the high-frequency word. The student re-reads it the next day.

Identify and Name Initial Consonant Ww RF.K.3a, RF.K.3c

CCSS: RF.K.3
Know and apply grade-level phonics and word analysis skills in decoding words both in isolation and in text.
a. Demonstrate basic knowledge of one-to-one letter-sound correspondences by producing the primary sound or many of the most frequent sounds for each consonant.
c. Read common high-frequency words by sight.

Lesson Objectives

- Identify and name the letter **Ww.**
- Produce the sound of letter **Ww**.
- Relate the sound /**w**/ to the letter **Ww**.
- Recognize initial sound /**w**/ in words/pictures.
- Read common high-frequency words: **have, are.**

Metacognitive Strategy
- Selective Auditory Attention

Academic Language
- letter name, letter sound, initial sound, high-frequency word

Additional Materials
- Sound Spelling Card **Ww**
- Poetry Poster "Worm"
- Blackline Masters 25, 26

Pre-Assess
Student's ability to recognize the sound represented by the targeted letter of the alphabet and to identify the letter used to represent the corresponding sound.

Introduce

As students participate in this lesson, they will identify the name and sound of the targeted letter and will identify the letter when the sound and name is given orally. They will apply their knowledge by recognizing the initial sound of the target letter using pictures. They will also apply the skill in context by reading decodable simple sentences that include high-frequency words.

State Learning Goal

Say: Today we will practice matching the sound and letter **w**.

Display Sound Spelling Card **Ww**.

Say: This is capital **W**. This is lowercase **w**.

Teach

Say: Letters represent sounds. We remember the sounds each letter makes. We use letters to write words we say. We use letters to read and write words.

Shared Reading

Use the poetry poster "Worm." Read the poem aloud emphasizing rhythm and rhyme, and target sound. Invite students to echo-read or chime in the rhyme on cue.

Phonemic Awareness

Show the picture of the sound/spelling card to review the sound.

Say: This is the **Ww** card. Listen to this sound /**w**/. Say it with me: /**w**/. Now say it on your own: /**w**/.

Display the poetry poster and read it aloud.

Sound-Spelling Correspondence

Show the letter.

Say: The way we write the sound /**w**/ is with the letter **w**. The letter **w** makes the sound /**w**/.

Ask: What is the name of the letter? (**w**) What sound does the letter make? /**w**/.

Model

Use BLM 25, Row 1.

Say: We will look at each picture. Say its name. If we hear the sound /**w**/ at the beginning of the word, we will circle the picture. If we do not hear the sound /**w**/ at the beginning, we will cross out the picture.

Ask: What do you see in the first picture? (**wig**) Do you hear the sound /**w**/ at the beginning of the word **wig**?

Say: Circle the letter **w**. If you do not hear the sound /**w**/ at the beginning of the word, then cross out the picture. Repeat with other words.

Practice

Use BLM 25, Row 2.

Say: *Look at the picture. Say its name. Write the letter.*

Ask: *What do you see in the second picture?* (**wax**) *Do you hear the sound* /**w**/ *at the beginning of the word* **wax**? *Write the letter* **w**. Repeat with other words.

Apply

Blend Words

Use BLM 25, Row 3.

Say: *Look at each letter and listen to the sound as I read:* /**w**/ /**e**/ /**d**/. *Your turn:* /**w**/ /**e**/ /**d**/.

Say: *Now we are going to blend the sounds together by stretching them out as we read them.* Point to each letter in a sweeping motion left to right /**weeed**/.

Ask: *What is the word?* (**wed**) Repeat with other words.

High-Frequency words

Use BLM 25, Row 4.

Say: *First, I will point to the word and read it. Then, you will point to the word and we will read it together. Next, I will read a word and you will point to it. Now, you will read the word and I will point to it. Let's write/trace the word as we spell it:* **are**.

Decodable Text

Use BLM 26, Row 1.

Say: *First, I will point to each word as I read the sentence. Then, you will point to each word and we will read together. Next, I will read the sentence and you will point to each word as I read. Now, you will point to each word as you read. Circle all the examples of the letter* **w** *you find in these sentences. Circle the words* **have** *and* **are** *in these sentences.*

Spelling

Use BLM 26 Row 2.

Say: *Now we can practice writing the sounds we hear in each word. Say one word at a time, stretching each sound. Write a letter for each sound you hear.*

Conclusion

Ask: *What did we learn today? What pictures/words will help you remember the sound* /**w**/ *and the letter* **w**?

Say: *We learned that the letter* **w** *makes the sound* /**w**/. *We wrote words using the letter* **w**.

Home Connection

Ask students to practice identifying initial sound /**w**/ and writing the letter **w** with a family member. Have students identify other words that begin with letter **w** with their family.

✔ Formative Assessment

If the student completes each task correctly, proceed to the next skill in the sequence. If not, refer to suggested Intervention 2.

Did the student...?	Intervention 2
Identify the names of the letters?	• Use physical rhythmic movements as the letter name is repeated. March while chanting the letter name. Move arms up and down. Sway from side to side.
Identify the sounds of the letters?	• Use alliteration, chants that repeat the sound several times, then a word that begins with the sound. Example: /**w**/ /**w**/ /**w**/ **wig**.
Produce the sounds of the letters?	• Use mirrors to show the movement of the mouth, tongue, and teeth as the sound is produced. • Use hand over mouth to explore movement of air as the sound is produced.
Recognize the beginning sounds?	• Use Elkonin boxes – student moves a token into the first box as the beginning sound of the word is said.
Write the letters?	• Write the letter; have students trace it. Create the letter with clay. • Discuss the letter features (lines, shape). Trace over the letter with multiple colors.
Know the names of the pictures?	• Tell students the name of the pictures; have students repeat them aloud. • Discuss the words and use each word in context.
Read high-frequency words?	• Create take-home word cards. Use a reward system to track words learned over time. The student uses the word in a sentence, and the teacher writes it down and highlights the high-frequency word. The student re-reads it the next day.

Identify and Name Initial Consonant Ll RF.K.3a, RF.K.3c

CCSS: RF.K.3
Know and apply grade-level phonics and word analysis skills in decoding words both in isolation and in text.
a. Demonstrate basic knowledge of one-to-one letter-sound correspondences by producing the primary sound or many of the most frequent sounds for each consonant.
c. Read common high-frequency words by sight.

Lesson Objectives

- Identify and name the letter **Ll**.
- Produce the sound of letter **Ll**.
- Relate the sound /l/ to the letter **Ll**.
- Recognize initial sound /l/ in words/pictures.
- Read common high-frequency words: **said, two.**

Metacognitive Strategy
- Selective Auditory Attention

Academic Language
- letter name, letter sound, initial sound, high-frequency word

Additional Materials
- Sound Spelling Card **Ll**
- Poetry Poster "Lenny Lion"
- Blackline Masters 27, 28

Pre-Assess
Student's ability to recognize the sound represented by the targeted letter of the alphabet and to identify the letter used to represent the corresponding sound.

Introduce

As students participate in this lesson, they will identify the name and sound of the targeted letter and will identify the letter when the sound and name is given orally. They will apply their knowledge by recognizing the initial sound of the target letter using pictures. They will also apply the skill in context by reading decodable simple sentences that include high-frequency words.

State Learning Goal

Say: *Today we will practice matching the sound and letter* **l**.

Display Sound Spelling Card **Ll**.

Say: *This is capital* **L**. *This is lowercase* **l**.

Teach

Say: *Letters represent sounds. We remember the sounds each letter makes. We use letters to write words we say. We use letters to read and write words.*

Shared Reading

Use the poetry poster "Lenny Lion." Read the poem aloud emphasizing rhythm and rhyme, and target sound. Invite students to echo-read or chime in the rhyme on cue.

Phonemic Awareness

Show the picture of the sound/spelling card to review the sound.

Say: *This is the* **Ll** *card. Listen to this sound* /l/. *Say it with me:* /l/ *Now say it on your own:* /l/.

Display the poetry poster and read it aloud.

Sound-Spelling Correspondence

Show the letter.

Say: *The way we write the sound* /l/ *is with the letter* **l**. *The letter* **l** *makes the sound* /l/.

Ask: *What is the name of the letter?* (**l**) *What sound does the letter make?* /l/.

Model

Use BLM 27, Row 1.

Say: *We will look at each picture. Say its name. If we hear the sound* /l/ *at the beginning of the word, we will circle the picture. If we do not hear the sound* /l/ *at the beginning, we will cross out the picture.*

Ask: *What do you see in the first picture?* (**lid**) *Do you hear the sound* /l/ *at the beginning of the word* **lid***?*

Say: *Circle the letter* **l**. *If you do not hear the sound* /l/ *at the beginning of the word, then cross out the picture.* Repeat with other words.

Practice

Use BLM 27, Row 2.

Say: *Look at the picture. Say its name. Write the letter.*

Ask: *What do you see in the second picture?* (**log**) *Do you hear the sound /l/ at the beginning of the word* **log**? *Write the letter* **l**. *Repeat with other words.*

Apply

Blend Words

Use BLM 27, Row 3.

Say: *Look at each letter and listen to the sound as I read: /l/ /a/ /p/. Your turn: /l/ /a/ /p/.*

Say: *Now we are going to blend the sounds together by stretching them out as we read them.* Point to each letter in a sweeping motion left to right /**lllaaap**/.

Ask: *What is the word?* (**lap**) *Repeat with other words.*

High-Frequency words

Use BLM 27, Row 4.

Say: *First, I will point to the word and read it. Then, you will point to the word and we will read it together. Next, I will read a word and you will point to it. Now, you will read the word and I will point to it. Let's write/trace the word as we spell it:* **said***.*

Decodable Text

Use BLM 28, Row 1.

Say: *First, I will point to each word as I read the sentence. Then, you will point to each word and we will read together. Next, I will read the sentence and you will point to each word as I read. Now, you will point to each word as you read. Circle all the examples of the letter* **l** *you find in these sentences. Circle the words* **said** *and* **two** *in these sentences.*

Spelling

Use BLM 28 Row 2.

Say: *Now we can practice writing the sounds we hear in each word. Say one word at a time, stretching each sound. Write a letter for each sound you hear.*

Conclusion

Ask: *What did we learn today? What pictures/words will help you remember the sound /l/ and the letter* **l**?

Say: *We learned that the letter* **l** *makes the sound /l/. We wrote words using the letter* **l***.*

Home Connection

Ask students to practice identifying initial sound /l/ and writing the letter **l** with a family member. Have students identify other words that begin with letter **l** with their family.

✔ Formative Assessment

If the student completes each task correctly, proceed to the next skill in the sequence. If not, refer to suggested Intervention 2.

Did the student…?	Intervention 2
Identify the names of the letters?	• Use physical rhythmic movements as the letter name is repeated. March while chanting the letter name. Move arms up and down. Sway from side to side.
Identify the sounds of the letters?	• Use alliteration, chants that repeat the sound several times, then a word that begins with the sound. Example: /l/ /l/ /l/ **lid**.
Produce the sounds of the letters?	• Use mirrors to show the movement of the mouth, tongue, and teeth as the sound is produced. • Use hand over mouth to explore movement of air as the sound is produced.
Recognize the beginning sounds?	• Use Elkonin boxes – student moves a token into the first box as the beginning sound of the word is said.
Write the letters?	• Write the letter; have students trace it. Create the letter with clay. • Discuss the letter features (lines, shape). Trace over the letter with multiple colors.
Know the names of the pictures?	• Tell students the name of the pictures; have students repeat them aloud. • Discuss the words and use each word in context.
Read high-frequency words?	• Create take-home word cards. Use a reward system to track words learned over time. The student uses the word in a sentence, and the teacher writes it down and highlights the high-frequency word. The student re-reads it the next day.

Identify and Name Initial Consonant Jj RF.K.3a, RF.K.3c

CCSS: RF.K.3
Know and apply grade-level phonics and word analysis skills in decoding words both in isolation and in text.
a. Demonstrate basic knowledge of one-to-one letter-sound correspondences by producing the primary sound or many of the most frequent sounds for each consonant.
c. Read common high-frequency words by sight.

Lesson Objectives

- Identify and name the letter **Jj.**
- Produce the sound of letter **Jj.**
- Relate the sound /**j**/ to the letter **Jj.**
- Recognize initial sound /**j**/ in words/pictures.
- Read common high-frequency words: **for, jump, one, have.**

Metacognitive Strategy
- Selective Auditory Attention

Academic Language
- letter name, letter sound, initial sound, high-frequency word

Additional Materials
- Sound Spelling Card **Jj**
- Poetry Poster "Jumping"
- Blackline Masters 29, 30

Pre-Assess
Student's ability to recognize the sound represented by the targeted letter of the alphabet and to identify the letter used to represent the corresponding sound.

Introduce

As students participate in this lesson, they will identify the name and sound of the targeted letter and will identify the letter when the sound and name is given orally. They will apply their knowledge by recognizing the initial sound of the target letter using pictures. They will also apply the skill in context by reading decodable simple sentences that include high-frequency words.

State Learning Goal

Say: *Today we will practice matching the sound and letter* **j**.

Display Sound Spelling Card **Jj**.

Say: *This is capital* **J**. *This is lowercase* **j**.

Teach

Say: *Letters represent sounds. We remember the sounds each letter makes. We use letters to write words we say. We use letters to read and write words.*

Shared Reading

Use the poetry poster "Jumping." Read the poem aloud emphasizing rhythm and rhyme, and target sound. Invite students to echo-read or chime in the rhyme on cue.

Phonemic Awareness

Show the picture of the sound/spelling card to review the sound.

Say: *This is the* **Jj** *card. Listen to this sound* /**j**/. *Say it with me:* /**j**/ *Now say it on your own:* /**j**/.

Display the poetry poster and read it aloud.

Sound-Spelling Correspondence

Show the letter.

Say: *The way we write the sound* /**j**/ *is with the letter* **j**. *The letter* **j** *makes the sound* /**j**/.

Ask: *What is the name of the letter?* (**j**) *What sound does the letter make?* /**j**/

Model

Use BLM 29, Row 1.

Say: *We will look at each picture. Say its name. If we hear the sound* /**j**/ *at the beginning of the word, we will circle the picture. If we do not hear the sound* /**j**/ *at the beginning, we will cross out the picture.*

Ask: *What do you see in the first picture?* (**jet**) *Do you hear the sound* /**j**/ *at the beginning of the word* **jet**?

Say: *Circle the letter* **j**. *If you do not hear the sound* /**j**/ *at the beginning of the word, then cross out the picture.* Repeat with other words.

Practice

Use BLM 29, Row 2.

Say: *Look at the picture. Say its name. Write the letter.*

Ask: *What do you see in the second picture?* (**jam**) *Do you hear the sound /j/ at the beginning of the word* **jam***? Write the letter* **j***. Repeat with other words.*

Apply

Blend Words

Use BLM 29, Row 3.

Say: *Look at each letter and listen to the sound as I read: /j/ /u/ /g/. Your turn: /j/ /u/ /g/.*

Say: *Now we are going to blend the sounds together by stretching them out as we read them.* Point to each letter in a sweeping motion left to right **/juuug/***.*

Ask: *What is the word?* (**jug**) *Repeat with other words.*

High-Frequency words

Use BLM 29, Row 4.

Say: *First, I will point to the word and read it. Then, you will point to the word and we will read it together. Next, I will read a word and you will point to it. Now, you will read the word and I will point to it. Let's write/trace the word as we spell it:* **jump***.*

Decodable Text

Use BLM 30, Row 1.

Say: *First, I will point to each word as I read the sentence. Then, you will point to each word and we will read together. Next, I will read the sentence and you will point to each word as I read. Now, you will point to each word as you read. Circle all the examples of the letter* **j** *you find in these sentences. Circle the words* **jump, have, one,** *and* **for** *in these sentences.*

Spelling

Use BLM 30 Row 2.

Say: *Now we can practice writing the sounds we hear in each word. Say one word at a time, stretching each sound. Write a letter for each sound you hear.*

Conclusion

Ask: *What did we learn today? What pictures/words will help you remember the sound /j/ and the letter* **j***?*

Say: *We learned that the letter* **j** *makes the sound /j/. We wrote words using the letter* **j***.*

©2017 Benchmark Education Company, LLC

Home Connection

Ask students to practice identifying initial sound /j/ and writing the letter **j** with a family member. Have students identify other words that begin with letter **j** with their family.

✔ Formative Assessment

If the student completes each task correctly, proceed to the next skill in the sequence. If not, refer to suggested Intervention 2.

Did the student…?	Intervention 2
Identify the names of the letters?	• Use physical rhythmic movements as the letter name is repeated. March while chanting the letter name. Move arms up and down. Sway from side to side.
Identify the sounds of the letters?	• Use alliteration, chants that repeat the sound several times, then a word that begins with the sound. Example: /j/ /j/ /j/ **jab**.
Produce the sounds of the letters?	• Use mirrors to show the movement of the mouth, tongue, and teeth as the sound is produced. • Use hand over mouth to explore movement of air as the sound is produced.
Recognize the beginning sounds?	• Use Elkonin boxes – student moves a token into the first box as the beginning sound of the word is said.
Write the letters?	• Write the letter; have students trace it. Create the letter with clay. • Discuss the letter features (lines, shape). Trace over the letter with multiple colors.
Know the names of the pictures?	• Tell students the name of the pictures; have students repeat them aloud. • Discuss the words and use each word in context.
Read high-frequency words?	• Create take-home word cards. Use a reward system to track words learned over time. The student uses the word in a sentence, and the teacher writes it down and highlights the high-frequency word. The student re-reads it the next day.

Identify and Name Initial Consonant Kk RF.K.3a, RF.K.3c

CCSS: RF.K.3
Know and apply grade-level phonics and word analysis skills in decoding words both in isolation and in text.
a. Demonstrate basic knowledge of one-to-one letter-sound correspondences by producing the primary sound or many of the most frequent sounds for each consonant.
c. Read common high-frequency words by sight.

Lesson Objectives

- Identify and name the letter **Kk.**
- Produce the sound of letter **Kk.**
- Relate the sound /**k**/ to the letter **Kk.**
- Recognize initial sound /**k**/ in words/pictures.
- Read common high-frequency words: **look, me.**

Metacognitive Strategy
- Selective Auditory Attention

Academic Language
- letter name, letter sound, initial sound, high-frequency word

Additional Materials
- Sound Spelling Card **Kk**
- Poetry Poster "King Karl's Kangaroo"
- Blackline Masters 31, 32

Pre-Assess
Student's ability to recognize the sound represented by the targeted letter of the alphabet and to identify the letter used to represent the corresponding sound.

Introduce

As students participate in this lesson, they will identify the name and sound of the targeted letter and will identify the letter when the sound and name is given orally. They will apply their knowledge by recognizing the initial sound of the target letter using pictures. They will also apply the skill in context by reading decodable simple sentences that include high-frequency words.

State Learning Goal

Say: *Today we will practice matching the sound and letter* **k**.

Display Sound Spelling Card **Kk**.

Say: *This is capital* **K**. *This is lowercase* **k**.

Teach

Say: *Letters represent sounds. We remember the sounds each letter makes. We use letters to write words we say. We use letters to read and write words.*

Shared Reading

Use the poetry poster "King Karl's Kangaroo." Read the poem aloud emphasizing rhythm and rhyme, and target sound. Invite students to echo-read or chime in the rhyme on cue.

Phonemic Awareness

Show the picture of the sound/spelling card to review the sound.

Say: *This is the* **Kk** *card. Listen to this sound* /**k**/. *Say it with me:* /**k**/ *Now say it on your own:* /**k**/.

Display the poetry poster and read it aloud.

Sound-Spelling Correspondence

Show the letter.

Say: *The way we write the sound* /**k**/ *is with the letter* **k**. *The letter* **k** *makes the sound* /**k**/.

Ask: *What is the name of the letter?* (**k**) *What sound does the letter make?* /**k**/.

Model

Use BLM 31, Row 1.

Say: *We will look at each picture. Say its name. If we hear the sound* /**k**/ *at the beginning of the word, we will circle the picture. If we do not hear the sound* /**k**/ *at the beginning, we will cross out the picture.*

Ask: *What do you see in the first picture?* (**kid**) *Do you hear the sound* /**k**/ *at the beginning of the word* **kid**?

Say: *Circle the letter* **k**. *If you do not hear the sound* /**k**/ *at the beginning of the word, then cross out the picture.* **Repeat with other words.**

Practice

Use BLM 31, Row 2.

Say: *Look at the picture. Say its name. Write the letter.*

Ask: *What do you see in the third picture?* (**key**) *Do you hear the sound /k/ at the beginning of the word* **key***? Write the letter* **k***.* Repeat with other words.

Apply

Blend Words

Use BLM 31, Row 3.

Say: *Look at each letter and listen to the sound as I read: /k/ /e/ /n/. Your turn: /k/ /e/ /n/.*

Say: *Now we are going to blend the sounds together by stretching them out as we read them.* Point to each letter in a sweeping motion left to right **/keeennn/**.

Ask: *What is the word?* (**Ken**) Repeat with other words.

High-Frequency words

Use BLM 31, Row 4.

Say: *First, I will point to the word and read it. Then, you will point to the word and we will read it together. Next, I will read a word and you will point to it. Now, you will read the word and I will point to it. Let's write/trace the word as we spell it:* **look***.*

Decodable Text

Use BLM 32, Row 1.

Say: *First, I will point to each word as I read the sentence. Then, you will point to each word and we will read together. Next, I will read the sentence and you will point to each word as I read. Now, you will point to each word as you read. Circle all the examples of the letter* **k** *you find in these sentences. Circle the words* **look** *and* **me** *in these sentences.*

Spelling

Use BLM 32 Row 2.

Say: *Now we can practice writing the sounds we hear in each word. Say one word at a time, stretching each sound. Write a letter for each sound you hear.*

Conclusion

Ask: *What did we learn today? What pictures/words will help you remember the sound /k/ and the letter* **k***?*

Say: *We learned that the letter* **k** *makes the sound /k/. We wrote words using the letter* **k***.*

Home Connection

Ask students to practice identifying initial sound /**k**/ and writing the letter **k** with a family member. Have students identify other words that begin with letter **k** with their family.

✔ Formative Assessment

If the student completes each task correctly, proceed to the next skill in the sequence. If not, refer to suggested Intervention 2.

Did the student…?	Intervention 2
Identify the names of the letters?	• Use physical rhythmic movements as the letter name is repeated. March while chanting the letter name. Move arms up and down. Sway from side to side.
Identify the sounds of the letters?	• Use alliteration, chants that repeat the sound several times, then a word that begins with the sound. Example: /**k**/ /**k**/ /**k**/ **kit**.
Produce the sounds of the letters?	• Use mirrors to show the movement of the mouth, tongue, and teeth as the sound is produced. • Use hand over mouth to explore movement of air as the sound is produced.
Recognize the beginning sounds?	• Use Elkonin boxes – student moves a token into the first box as the beginning sound of the word is said.
Write the letters?	• Write the letter; have students trace it. Create the letter with clay. • Discuss the letter features (lines, shape). Trace over the letter with multiple colors.
Know the names of the pictures?	• Tell students the name of the pictures; have students repeat them aloud. • Discuss the words and use each word in context.
Read high-frequency words?	• Create take-home word cards. Use a reward system to track words learned over time. The student uses the word in a sentence, and the teacher writes it down and highlights the high-frequency word. The student re-reads it the next day.

Identify and Name Initial Consonant Yy RF.K.3a, RF.K.3c

CCSS: RF.K.3
Know and apply grade-level phonics and word analysis skills in decoding words both in isolation and in text.
a. Demonstrate basic knowledge of one-to-one letter-sound correspondences by producing the primary sound or many of the most frequent sounds for each consonant.
c. Read common high-frequency words by sight.

Lesson Objectives

- Identify and name the letter **Yy.**
- Produce the sound of letter **Yy.**
- Relate the sound /**y**/ to the letter **Yy.**
- Recognize initial sound /**y**/ in words/pictures.
- Read common high-frequency words: **come, here.**

Metacognitive Strategy
- Selective Auditory Attention

Academic Language
- letter name, letter sound, initial sound, high-frequency word

Additional Materials
- Sound Spelling Card **Yy**
- Poetry Poster "Yellow"
- Blackline Masters 33, 34

Pre-Assess
Student's ability to recognize the sound represented by the targeted letter of the alphabet and to identify the letter used to represent the corresponding sound.

Introduce

As students participate in this lesson, they will identify the name and sound of the targeted letter and will identify the letter when the sound and name is given orally. They will apply their knowledge by recognizing the initial sound of the target letter using pictures. They will also apply the skill in context by reading decodable simple sentences that include high-frequency words.

State Learning Goal

Say: *Today we will practice matching the sound and letter* **y**.

Display Sound Spelling Card **Yy**.

Say: *This is capital* **Y**. *This is lowercase* **y**.

Teach

Say: *Letters represent sounds. We remember the sounds each letter makes. We use letters to write words we say. We use letters to read and write words.*

Shared Reading

Use the poetry poster "Yellow." Read the poem aloud emphasizing rhythm and rhyme, and target sound. Invite students to echo-read or chime in the rhyme on cue.

Phonemic Awareness

Show the picture of the sound/spelling card to review the sound.

Say: *This is the* **Yy** *card. Listen to this sound* /**y**/. *Say it with me:* /**y**/ *Now say it on your own:* /**y**/.

Display the poetry poster and read it aloud.

Sound-Spelling Correspondence

Show the letter.

Say: *The way we write the sound* /**y**/ *is with the letter* **y**. *The letter* **y** *makes the sound* /**y**/.

Ask: *What is the name of the letter?* (**y**) *What sound does the letter make?* /**y**/.

Model

Use BLM 33, Row 1.

Say: *We will look at each picture. Say its name. If we hear the sound* /**y**/ *at the beginning of the word, we will circle the picture. If we do not hear the sound* /**y**/ *at the beginning, we will cross out the picture.*

Ask: *What do you see in the first picture?* (**yes**) *Do you hear the sound* /**y**/ *at the beginning of the word* **yes**?

Say: *Circle the letter* **y**. *If you do not hear the sound* /**y**/ *at the beginning of the word, then cross out the picture.* **Repeat with other words.**

Practice

Use BLM 33, Row 2.

Say: *Look at the picture. Say its name. Write the letter.*

Ask: *What do you see in the second picture?* (**yak**) *Do you hear the sound /y/ at the beginning of the word* **yak**? *Write the letter* **y**. *Repeat with other words.*

Apply

Blend Words

Use BLM 33, Row 3.

Say: *Look at each letter and listen to the sound as I read: /y/ /a/ /m/. Your turn: /y/ /a/ /m/.*

Say: *Now we are going to blend the sounds together by stretching them out as we read them.* Point to each letter in a sweeping motion left to right /**yyyaaammm**/.

Ask: *What is the word?* (**yam**) *Repeat with other words.*

High-Frequency words

Use BLM 33, Row 4.

Say: *First, I will point to the word and read it. Then, you will point to the word and we will read it together. Next, I will read a word and you will point to it. Now, you will read the word and I will point to it. Let's write/trace the word as we spell it:* **here***.*

Decodable Text

Use BLM 34, Row 1.

Say: *First, I will point to each word as I read the sentence. Then, you will point to each word and we will read together. Next, I will read the sentence and you will point to each word as I read. Now, you will point to each word as you read. Circle all the examples of the letter* **y** *you find in these sentences. Circle the words* **come** *and* **here** *in these sentences.*

Spelling

Use BLM 34 Row 2.

Say: *Now we can practice writing the sounds we hear in each word. Say one word at a time, stretching each sound. Write a letter for each sound you hear.*

Conclusion

Ask: *What did we learn today? What pictures/words will help you remember the sound /y/ and the letter* **y**?

Say: *We learned that the letter* **y** *makes the sound /y/. We wrote words using the letter* **y**.

Home Connection

Ask students to practice identifying initial sound /y/ and writing the letter y with a family member. Have students identify other words that begin with letter y with their family.

✔ Formative Assessment

If the student completes each task correctly, proceed to the next skill in the sequence. If not, refer to suggested Intervention 2.

Did the student...?	Intervention 2
Identify the names of the letters?	• Use physical rhythmic movements as the letter name is repeated. March while chanting the letter name. Move arms up and down. Sway from side to side.
Identify the sounds of the letters?	• Use alliteration, chants that repeat the sound several times, then a word that begins with the sound. Example: /y/ /y/ /y/ **yet**.
Produce the sounds of the letters?	• Use mirrors to show the movement of the mouth, tongue, and teeth as the sound is produced. • Use hand over mouth to explore movement of air as the sound is produced.
Recognize the beginning sounds?	• Use Elkonin boxes – student moves a token into the first box as the beginning sound of the word is said.
Write the letters?	• Write the letter; have students trace it. Create the letter with clay. • Discuss the letter features (lines, shape). Trace over the letter with multiple colors.
Know the names of the pictures?	• Tell students the name of the pictures; have students repeat them aloud. • Discuss the words and use each word in context.
Read high-frequency words?	• Create take-home word cards. Use a reward system to track words learned over time. The student uses the word in a sentence, and the teacher writes it down and highlights the high-frequency word. The student re-reads it the next day.

Identify and Name Initial Consonant Vv RF.K.3a, RF.K.3c

CCSS: RF.K.3
Know and apply grade-level phonics and word analysis skills in decoding words both in isolation and in text.
a. Demonstrate basic knowledge of one-to-one letter-sound correspondences by producing the primary sound or many of the most frequent sounds for each consonant.
c. Read common high-frequency words by sight.

Lesson Objectives

- Identify and name the letter **Vv.**
- Produce the sound of letter **Vv.**
- Relate the sound /**v**/ to the letter **Vv.**
- Recognize initial sound /**v**/ in words/pictures.
- Read common high-frequency words: **here, look, said, come.**

Metacognitive Strategy
- Selective Auditory Attention

Academic Language
- letter name, letter sound, initial sound, high-frequency word

Additional Materials
- Sound Spelling Card **Vv**
- Poetry Poster "Violins and Violets"
- Blackline Masters 35, 36

Pre-Assess
Student's ability to recognize the sound represented by the targeted letter of the alphabet and to identify the letter used to represent the corresponding sound.

Introduce

As students participate in this lesson, they will identify the name and sound of the targeted letter and will identify the letter when the sound and name is given orally. They will apply their knowledge by recognizing the initial sound of the target letter using pictures. They will also apply the skill in context by reading decodable simple sentences that include high-frequency words.

State Learning Goal

Say: Today we will practice matching the sound and letter **v**.

Display Sound Spelling Card **Vv**.

Say: This is capital **V**. This is lowercase **v**.

Teach

Say: Letters represent sounds. We remember the sounds each letter makes. We use letters to write words we say. We use letters to read and write words.

Shared Reading

Use the poetry poster "Violins and Violets." Read the poem aloud emphasizing rhythm and rhyme, and target sound. Invite students to echo-read or chime in the rhyme on cue.

Phonemic Awareness

Show the picture of the sound/spelling card to review the sound.

Say: This is the **Vv** card. Listen to this sound /**v**/. Say it with me: /**v**/ Now say it on your own: /**v**/.

Display the poetry poster and read it aloud.

Sound-Spelling Correspondence

Show the letter.

Say: The way we write the sound /**v**/ is with the letter **v**. The letter **v** makes the sound /**v**/.

Ask: What is the name of the letter? (**v**) What sound does the letter make? /**v**/.

Model

Use BLM 35, Row 1.

Say: We will look at each picture. Say its name. If we hear the sound /**v**/ at the beginning of the word, we will circle the picture. If we do not hear the sound /**v**/ at the beginning, we will cross out the picture.

Ask: Who do you see in the first picture? (**Val**) Do you hear the sound /**v**/ at the beginning of the word **Val**?

Say: Circle the letter **v**. If you do not hear the sound /**v**/ at the beginning of the word, then cross out the picture. Repeat with other words.

Practice

Use BLM 35, Row 2.

Say: *Look at the picture. Say its name. Write the letter.*

Ask: *Who do you see in the second picture?* (**Vic**) *Do you hear the sound /**v**/ at the beginning of the word* **Vic**? *Write the letter* **v**. Repeat with other words.

Apply

Blend Words

Use BLM 35, Row 3.

Say: *Look at each letter and listen to the sound as I read: /**v**/ /**a**/ /**n**/. Your turn: /**v**/ /**a**/ /**n**/.*

Say: *Now we are going to blend the sounds together by stretching them out as we read them.* Point to each letter in a sweeping motion left to right /**vvvaaannn**/.

Ask: *What is the word?* (**van**) Repeat with other words.

High-Frequency words

Use BLM 35, Row 4.

Say: *First, I will point to the word and read it. Then, you will point to the word and we will read it together. Next, I will read a word and you will point to it. Now, you will read the word and I will point to it. Let's write/trace the word as we spell it:* **here**.

Decodable Text

Use BLM 36, Row 1.

Say: *First, I will point to each word as I read the sentence. Then, you will point to each word and we will read together. Next, I will read the sentence and you will point to each word as I read. Now, you will point to each word as you read. Circle all the examples of the letter* **v** *you find in these sentences. Circle the words* **here, look, said,** *and* **come** *in these sentences.*

Spelling

Use BLM 36 Row 2.

Say: *Now we can practice writing the sounds we hear in each word. Say one word at a time, stretching each sound. Write a letter for each sound you hear.*

Conclusion

Ask: *What did we learn today? What pictures/words will help you remember the sound /**v**/ and the letter* **v**?

Say: *We learned that the letter* **v** *makes the sound /**v**/. We wrote words using the letter* **v**.

Home Connection

Ask students to practice identifying initial sound /**v**/ and writing the letter **v** with a family member. Have students identify other words that begin with letter **v** with their family.

✔ Formative Assessment

If the student completes each task correctly, proceed to the next skill in the sequence. If not, refer to suggested Intervention 2.

Did the student…?	Intervention 2
Identify the names of the letters?	• Use physical rhythmic movements as the letter name is repeated. March while chanting the letter name. Move arms up and down. Sway from side to side.
Identify the sounds of the letters?	• Use alliteration, chants that repeat the sound several times, then a word that begins with the sound. Example: /**v**/ /**v**/ /**v**/ **vet**.
Produce the sounds of the letters?	• Use mirrors to show the movement of the mouth, tongue, and teeth as the sound is produced. • Use hand over mouth to explore movement of air as the sound is produced.
Recognize the beginning sounds?	• Use Elkonin boxes – student moves a token into the first box as the beginning sound of the word is said.
Write the letters?	• Write the letter; have students trace it. Create the letter with clay. • Discuss the letter features (lines, shape). Trace over the letter with multiple colors.
Know the names of the pictures?	• Tell students the name of the pictures; have students repeat them aloud. • Discuss word and use each word in context.
Read high-frequency words?	• Create take-home word cards. Use a reward system to track words learned over time. The student uses the word in a sentence, and the teacher writes it down and highlights the high-frequency word. The student re-reads it the next day.

Identify and Name Initial Consonant Qq RF.K.3a, RF.K.3c

CCSS: RF.K.3
Know and apply grade-level phonics and word analysis skills in decoding words both in isolation and in text.
a. Demonstrate basic knowledge of one-to-one letter-sound correspondences by producing the primary sound or many of the most frequent sounds for each consonant.
c. Read common high-frequency words by sight.

Lesson Objectives

- Identify and name the letter **Qq.**
- Produce the sound of letter **Qq**.
- Relate the sound /**kw**/ to the letter **Qq**.
- Recognize initial sound /**kw**/ in words/pictures.
- Read common high-frequency words: **said, come, here, have.**

Metacognitive Strategy
- Selective Auditory Attention

Academic Language
- letter name, letter sound, initial sound, high-frequency word

Additional Materials
- Sound Spelling Card **Qq**
- Poetry Poster "The Queen's Nap"
- Blackline Masters 37, 38

Pre-Assess
Student's ability to recognize the sound represented by the targeted letter of the alphabet and to identify the letter used to represent the corresponding sound.

Introduce

As students participate in this lesson, they will identify the name and sound of the targeted letter and will identify the letter when the sound and name is given orally. They will apply their knowledge by recognizing the initial sound of the target letter using pictures. They will also apply the skill in context by reading decodable simple sentences that include high-frequency words.

State Learning Goal

Say: *Today we will practice matching the sound and letter* **q**.

Display Sound Spelling Card **Qq**.

Say: *This is capital* **Q**. *This is lowercase* **q**.

Teach

Say: *Letters represent sounds. We remember the sounds each letter makes. We use letters to write words we say. We use letters to read and write words.*

Shared Reading

Use the poetry poster "The Queen's Nap." Read the poem aloud emphasizing rhythm and rhyme, and target sound. Invite students to echo-read or chime in the rhyme on cue.

Phonemic Awareness

Show the picture of the sound/spelling card to review the sound.

Say: *This is the* **Qq** *card. Listen to this sound* /**kw**/. *Say it with me:* /**kw**/. *Now say it on your own:* /**kw**/.

Display the poetry poster and read it aloud.

Sound-Spelling Correspondence

Show the letter.

Say: *The way we write the sound* /**kw**/ *is with the letter* **q** *and the letter* **u**. *The letters* **q** *and* **u** *makes the sound* /**kw**/.

Ask: *What is the name of the letter?* (**q**) *What sound do the letters* **qu** *make?* /**kw**/.

Model

Use BLM 37, Row 1.

Say: *We will look at each picture. Say its name. If we hear the sound* /**kw**/ *at the beginning of the word, we will circle the picture. If we do not hear the sound* /**kw**/ *at the beginning, we will cross out the picture.*

Ask: *What do you see in the first picture?* (*a* **quiz**) *Do you hear the sound* /**kw**/ *at the beginning of the word* **quiz**?

Say: *Circle the letter* **q**. *If you do not hear the sound* /**kw**/ *at the beginning of the word, then cross out the picture.* Repeat with other words.

Practice

Use BLM 37, Row 2.

Say: *Look at the picture. Say its name. Write the letter.*

Ask: *Who do you see in the first picture?* (**Quin**) *Do you hear the sound /****kw****/ at the beginning of the word* **Quin**? *Write the letters* **qu**. Repeat with other words.

Apply

Blend Words

Use BLM 37, Row 3.

Say: *Look at each letter and listen to the sound as I read: /****kw****/ /****i****/ /****t****/. Your turn: /****kw****/ /****i****/ /****t****/.*

Say: *Now we are going to blend the sounds together by stretching them out as we read them.* Point to each letter in a sweeping motion left to right /**kwiiit**/.

Ask: *What is the word?* (**quit**) Repeat with other words.

High-Frequency words

Use BLM 37, Row 4.

Say: *First, I will point to the word and read it. Then, you will point to the word and we will read it together. Next, I will read a word and you will point to it. Now, you will read the word and I will point to it. Let's write/trace the word as we spell it:* **said**.

Decodable Text

Use BLM 38, Row 1.

Say: *First, I will point to each word as I read the sentence. Then, you will point to each word and we will read together. Next, I will read the sentence and you will point to each word as I read. Now, you will point to each word as you read. Circle all the examples of the letter* **q** *you find in these sentences. Circle the words* **said, come, here,** *and* **have** *in these sentences.*

Spelling

Use BLM 38, Row 2.

Say: *Now we can practice writing the sounds we hear in each word. Say one word at a time, stretching each sound. Write a letter for each sound you hear.*

Conclusion

Ask: *What did we learn today? What pictures/words will help you remember the sound /****kw****/ and the letter* **q**?

Say: *We learned that the letter* **q** *with the letter* **u** *makes the sound /****kw****/. We wrote words using the letter* **q**.

Home Connection

Ask students to practice identifying initial sound /**kw**/ and writing the letter **q** with a family member. Have students identify other words that begin with letter **q** with their family.

✔ Formative Assessment

If the student completes each task correctly, proceed to the next skill in the sequence. If not, refer to suggested Intervention 2.

Did the student…?	Intervention 2
Identify the names of the letters?	• Use physical rhythmic movements as the letter name is repeated. March while chanting the letter name. Move arms up and down. Sway from side to side.
Identify the sounds of the letters?	• Use alliteration, chants that repeat the sound several times, then a word that begins with the sound. Example: /**kw**/ /**kw**/ /**kw**/ **quit**.
Produce the sounds of the letters?	• Use mirrors to show the movement of the mouth, tongue, and teeth as the sound is produced. • Use hand over mouth to explore movement of air as the sound is produced.
Recognize the beginning sounds?	• Use Elkonin boxes – student moves a token into the first box as the beginning sound of the word is said.
Write the letters?	• Write the letter; have students trace it. Create the letter with clay. • Discuss the letter features (lines, shape). Trace over the letter with multiple colors.
Know the names of the pictures?	• Tell students the name of the pictures; have students repeat them aloud. • Discuss the words and use each word in context.
Read high-frequency words?	• Create take-home word cards. Use a reward system to track words learned over time. The student uses the word in a sentence, and the teacher writes it down and highlights the high-frequency word. The student re-reads it the next day.

Identify and Name Initial Consonant Zz RF.K.3a, RF.K.3c

CCSS: RF.K.3
Know and apply grade-level phonics and word analysis skills in decoding words both in isolation and in text.
a. Demonstrate basic knowledge of one-to-one letter-sound correspondences by producing the primary sound or many of the most frequent sounds for each consonant.
c. Read common high-frequency words by sight.

Lesson Objectives

- Identify and name the letter **Zz.**
- Produce the sound of letter **Zz.**
- Relate the sound /**z**/ to the letter **Zz.**
- Recognize initial sound /**z**/ in words/pictures.
- Read common high-frequency words: **to, my.**

Metacognitive Strategy
- Selective Auditory Attention

Academic Language
- letter name, letter sound, initial sound, high-frequency word

Additional Materials
- Sound Spelling Card **Zz**
- Poetry Poster "Zigzag"
- Blackline Masters 39, 40

Pre-Assess
Student's ability to recognize the sound represented by the targeted letter of the alphabet and to identify the letter used to represent the corresponding sound.

Introduce

As students participate in this lesson, they will identify the name and sound of the targeted letter and will identify the letter when the sound and name is given orally. They will apply their knowledge by recognizing the initial sound of the target letter using pictures. They will also apply the skill in context by reading decodable simple sentences that include high-frequency words.

State Learning Goal

Say: Today we will practice matching the sound and letter **z**

Display Sound Spelling Card **Zz**.

Say: This is capital **Z**. This is lowercase **z**

Teach

Say: Letters represent sounds. We remember the sounds each letter makes. We use letters to write words we say. We use letters to read and write words.

Shared Reading

Use the poetry poster "Zigzag." Read the poem aloud emphasizing rhythm and rhyme, and target sound. Invite students to echo-read or chime in the rhyme on cue.

Phonemic Awareness

Show the picture of the sound/spelling card to review the sound.

Say: This is the **Zz** card. Listen to this sound /**z**/. Say it with me: /**z**/ Now say it on your own: /**z**/.

Display the poetry poster and read it aloud.

Sound-Spelling Correspondence

Show the letter.

Say: The way we write the sound /**z**/ is with the letter **z** The letter **z** makes the sound /**z**/.

Ask: What is the name of the letter? (**z**) What sound does the letter make? /**z**/

Model

Use BLM 39, Row 1.

Say: We will look at each picture. Say its name. If we hear the sound /**z**/ at the beginning of the word, we will circle the picture. If we do not hear the sound /**z**/ at the beginning, we will cross out the picture.

Ask: What do you see in the first picture? (**zap**) Do you hear the sound /**z**/ at the beginning of the word **zap**?

Say: Circle the letter **z**. If you do not hear the sound /**z**/ at the beginning of the word, then cross out the picture. Repeat with other words.

Practice

Use BLM 39, Row 2.

Say: *Look at the picture. Say its name. Write the letter.*

Ask: *What do you see in the first picture?* (**zip**) *Do you hear the sound /z/ at the beginning of the word* **zip**? *Write the letter* **z** Repeat with other words.

Apply

Blend Words

Use BLM 39, Row 3.

Say: *Look at each letter and listen to the sound as I read: /z/ /a/ /k/. Your turn: /z/ /a/ /k/.*

Say: *Now we are going to blend the sounds together by stretching them out as we read them.* Point to each letter in a sweeping motion left to right /**zzzaaak**/.

Ask: *What is the word?* (**zak**). Repeat with other words.

High-Frequency words

Use BLM 39, Row 4.

Say: *First, I will point to the word and read it. Then, you will point to the word and we will read it together. Next, I will read a word and you will point to it. Now, you will read the word and I will point to it. Let's write/trace the word as we spell it:* **my**.

Decodable Text

Use BLM 40, Row 1.

Say: *First, I will point to each word as I read the sentence. Then, you will point to each word and we will read together. Next, I will read the sentence and you will point to each word as I read. Now, you will point to each word as you read. Circle all the examples of the letter* **z** *you find in these sentences. Circle the words* **to** *and* **my** *in these sentences.*

Spelling

Use BLM 40 Row 2.

Say: *Now we can practice writing the sounds we hear in each word. Say one word at a time, stretching each sound. Write a letter for each sound you hear.*

Conclusion

Ask: *What did we learn today? What pictures/words will help you remember the sound /z/ and the letter* **z**?

Say: *We learned that the letter* **z** *makes the sound /z/. We wrote words using the letter* **z**.

Home Connection

Ask students to practice identifying initial sound /**z**/ and writing the letter **z** with a family member. Have students identify other words that begin with letter **z** with their family.

✔ Formative Assessment

If the student completes each task correctly, proceed to the next skill in the sequence. If not, refer to suggested Intervention 2.

Did the student…?	Intervention 2
Identify the names of the letters?	• Use physical rhythmic movements as the letter name is repeated. March while chanting the letter name. Move arms up and down. Sway from side to side.
Identify the sounds of the letters?	• Use alliteration, chants that repeat the sound several times, then a word that begins with the sound. Example: /z/ /z/ /z/ **zig**.
Produce the sounds of the letters?	• Use mirrors to show the movement of the mouth, tongue, and teeth as the sound is produced. • Use hand over mouth to explore movement of air as the sound is produced.
Recognize the beginning sounds?	• Use Elkonin boxes – student moves a token into the first box as the beginning sound of the word is said.
Write the letters?	• Write the letter; have students trace it. Create the letter with clay. • Discuss the letter features (lines, shape). Trace over the letter with multiple colors.
Know the names of the pictures?	• Tell students the name of the pictures; have students repeat them aloud. • Discuss the words and use each word in context.
Read high-frequency words?	• Create take-home word cards. Use a reward system to track words learned over time. The student uses the word in a sentence, and the teacher writes it down and highlights the high-frequency word. The student re-reads it the next day.

Identify and Name Final Consonant Mm RF.K.3a, RF.K.3c

CCSS: RF.K.3
Know and apply grade-level phonics and word analysis skills in decoding words both in isolation and in text.
a. Demonstrate basic knowledge of one-to-one letter-sound correspondences by producing the primary sound or many of the most frequent sounds for each consonant.
c. Read common high-frequency words by sight.

Lesson Objectives

- Identify and name the letter **Mm**
- Produce the sound of letter **Mm**
- Relate the sound /**m**/ to the letter **Mm**
- Recognize final sound /**m**/ in words/pictures
- Read common high-frequency words: **I**

Metacognitive Strategy
- Selective Auditory Attention
- Imagery
- Auditory Representation

Academic Language
- letter name, letter sound, initial sound, final sound, ending sound, high-frequency word

Additional Materials
- Sound Spelling Card **Mm**
- Blackline Masters 41, 42

Pre-Assess
Student's ability to recognize the sound represented by the targeted letter of the alphabet and to identify the letter used to represent the corresponding sound in final position.

Introduce

As students participate in this lesson, they will identify the name and sound of the targeted letter and will identify the letter when the sound and name is given orally. Students will apply their knowledge by recognizing the final, or ending, sound of the target letter using pictures. Students will apply the skill in context by reading decodable simple sentences that include high-frequency words.

State Learning Goal

Say: *Today we will practice listening to the sound /**m**/ that the letter **m** makes at the **end** of words.*

Teach

Say: *Letters represent sounds. We remember the sounds each letter makes. We use letters to write words we say. We use letters to read and write words.*

Phonemic Awareness

Show the picture of the sound/spelling card to review the sound.

Say: *Listen to this sound /**m**/. Say it with me: **m**. Say it on your own: **m**.*

Sound-Spelling Correspondence
Show the letter.

Say: *The way we write the sound /**m**/ is with the letter **m**. The letter **m** makes the sound /**m**/.*

Ask: *What is the name of the letter? (**m**) What sound does the letter make? /**m**/*

Model
Use BLM 41, Row 1.

Say: *We will look at each picture. Say its name. If we hear the sound /**m**/ at the end of the word, we will circle the picture. If we do not hear the sound /**m**/ at the end, we will cross out the picture.*

Ask: *Who do you see in the first picture? (**Mom**) Do you hear the sound /**m**/ at the end of the word **Mom**?*

Say: *Circle the letter **m**. If you do not hear the sound /**m**/ at the end of the word, then cross out the picture.*

Practice
Use BLM 41, Row 2.

Say: *Look at the picture. Say its name. Write the letter.*

Ask: *Who does the first picture show? (**Sam**) Do you hear the sound /**m**/ at the end of the word **Sam**? Write the letter **m**. Repeat with other words.*

Apply

Blend Words
Use BLM 41, Row 3.

Say: *Look at each letter and listen to the sound as I read.* /**h**/ /**e**/ /**m**/. *Your turn:* /**h**/ /**e**/ /**m**/.

Say: *Now we are going to blend the sounds together by stretching them out as we read them.* Point to each letter in a sweeping motion left to right /**heeemmm**/.

Ask: *What is the word?* (**hem**). *Repeat with other words.*

High-Frequency words
Use BLM 41, Row 4.

Say: *First, I will point to the word and read it. Then, you will point to the word and we will read it together. Next, I will read a word and you will point to it. Now, you will read the word and I will point to it. Let's write/trace the word as we spell it:* **I**.

Decodable Text
Use BLM 42, Row 1.

Say: *First, I will point to each word as I read the sentence. Then, you will point to each word and we will read together. Next, I will read the sentence and you will point to each word as I read. Now, you will point to each word as you read. Circle all the examples of the letter* **m** *you can find in these sentences. Circle the word* **I** *in the sentences.*

Spelling
Use BLM 42, Row 2.

Say: *Now we can practice writing the sounds we hear in each word. Say one word at a time, stretching each sound. Write a letter for each sound you hear.*

Conclusion

Ask: *What did we learn today? What pictures/words will help you remember the sound* /**m**/ *and the letter* **m** *at the end of a word?*

Say: *We learned that the letter* **m** *makes the sound* /**m**/. *We wrote words using the letter* **m** *at the end.*

Home Connection
Encourage students to practice identifying the final sound /**m**/ and writing the letter **m** with a family member. Encourage students to identify other words that end with letter **m** with their family.

✔ Formative Assessment

If the student completes each task correctly, proceed to the next skill in the sequence. If not, refer to suggested Intervention 2.

Did the student…?	Intervention 2
Identify the names of the letters?	• Use physical rhythmic movements as the letter name is repeated. March while chanting the letter name. Move arms up and down. Sway from side to side.
Identify the sounds of the letters?	• Say words with the target sound in final position, emphasizing the sound. Example: **bummm.**
Produce the sounds of the letters?	• Use mirrors to show the movement of the mouth, tongue, and teeth as the sound is produced. • Use hand over mouth to explore movement of air as the sound is produced.
Recognize the final sounds?	• Use Elkonin boxes – student moves a token into the last box as the final sound of the word is said.
Write the letters?	• Write the letter; have students trace it. Create the letter with clay. • Discuss the letter features (lines, shape). Trace over the letter with multiple colors.
Know the names of the pictures?	• Tell students the name of the pictures; have students repeat them aloud. • Discuss the words and use each word in context.
Read high-frequency words?	• Create take-home word cards. Use a reward system to track words learned over time. The The student uses the word in a sentence, and the teacher writes it down and highlights the high-frequency word. The student re-reads it the next day.

Identify and Name Final Consonant Tt RF.K.3a, RF.K.3c

CCSS: RF.K.3
Know and apply grade-level phonics and word analysis skills in decoding words both in isolation and in text.
a. Demonstrate basic knowledge of one-to-one letter-sound correspondences by producing the primary sound or many of the most frequent sounds for each consonant.
c. Read common high-frequency words by sight.

Introduce

As students participate in this lesson, they will identify the name and sound of the targeted letter and will identify the letter when the sound and name is given orally. Students will apply their knowledge by recognizing the final, or ending, sound of the target letter using pictures. Students will apply the skill in context by reading decodable simple sentences that include high-frequency words.

State Learning Goal

Say: *Today we will practice listening to the sound /t/ that the letter t makes at the end of words.*

Teach

Say: *Letters represent sounds. We remember the sounds each letter makes. We use letters to write words we say. We use letters to read and write words.*

Phonemic Awareness

Show the picture of the sound/spelling card to review the sound.

Say: *Listen to this sound /t/. Say it with me:* **t** *Say it on your own:* **t**.

Sound-Spelling Correspondence

Show the letter.

Say: *The way we write the sound /t/ is with the letter* **t**. *The letter* **t** *makes the sound /t/.*

Ask: *What is the name of the letter?* **t** *What sound does the letter make? /t/.*

Model

Use BLM 43, Row 1.

Say: *We will look at each picture. Say its name. If we hear the sound /t/ at the end of the word, we will circle the letter* **t**. *If we do not hear the sound /t/ at the end, we will cross out the picture.*

Ask: *What do you see in the first picture?* (**mat**) *Do you hear the sound /t/ at the end of the word* **mat**?

Say: *Circle the picture. If you do not hear the sound /t/ at the end of the word, then cross out the picture.*

Practice

Use BLM 43, Row 2.

Say: *Look at the picture. Say its name. Write the letter.*

Ask: *What does the second picture show?* (**cat**) *Do you hear the sound /t/ at the end of the word* **cat**? *Write the letter* **t**. *Repeat with other words.*

Lesson Objectives

- Identify and name the letter **t**
- Produce the sound of letter **t**
- Relate the sound /t/ to the letter **t**
- Recognize final sound **t** in words/pictures
- Read common high-frequency words: **see, go**

Metacognitive Strategy
- Selective Auditory Attention
- Imagery
- Auditory Representation

Academic Language
- letter name, letter sound, initial sound, final sound, ending sound, high-frequency word

Additional Materials
- Sound Spelling Card **Tt**
- Blackline Masters 43, 44

Pre-Assess
Student's ability to recognize the sound represented by the targeted letter of the alphabet and to identify the letter used to represent the corresponding sound in final position.

Apply

Blend Words
Use BLM 43, Row 3.

Say: *Look at each letter and listen to the sound as I read. /**h**/ /**a**/ /**t**/. Your turn: /**h**/ /**a**/ /**t**/*

Say: *Now we are going to blend the sounds together by stretching them out as we read them.* Point to each letter in a sweeping motion left to right /**haaat**/.

Ask: *What is the word?* (**hat**) Repeat with other words.

High-Frequency words
Use BLM 43, Row 4.

Say: *First, I will point to the word and read it. Then, you will point to the word and we will read it together. Next, I will read a word and you will point to it. Now, you will read the word and I will point to it. Let's write/trace the word as we spell it:* **see.**

Decodable Text
Use BLM 44, Row 1.

Say: *First, I will point to each word as I read the sentence. Then, you will point to each word and we will read together. Next, I will read the sentence and you will point to each word as I read. Now, you will point to each word as you read. Circle all the examples of the letter* **t** *you can find in these sentences. Circle the words* **see** *and* **go** *in the sentences.*

Spelling
Use BLM 44, Row 2.

Say: *Now we can practice writing the sounds we hear in each word. Say one word at a time, stretching each sound. Write a letter for each sound you hear.*

Conclusion

Ask: *What did we learn today? What pictures/words will help you remember the sound /**t**/ and the letter* **t** *at the end of a word?*

Say: *We learned that the letter* **t** *makes the sound /**t**/. We wrote words using the letter* **t** *at the end.*

Home Connection
Encourage students to practice identifying the final sound /**t**/ and writing the letter **t** with a family member. Encourage students to identify other words that end with letter **t** with their family.

✔ Formative Assessment

If the student completes each task correctly, proceed to the next skill in the sequence. If not, refer to suggested Intervention 2.

Did the student…?	Intervention 2
Identify the names of the letters?	• Use physical rhythmic movements as the letter name is repeated. March while chanting the letter name. Move arms up and down. Sway from side to side.
Identify the sounds of the letters?	• Say words with the target sound in final position by repeating the words three times. Example: **cat, cat, cat.**
Produce the sounds of the letters?	• Use mirrors to show the movement of the mouth, tongue, and teeth as the sound is produced. • Use hand over mouth to explore movement of air as the sound is produced.
Recognize the final sounds?	• Use Elkonin boxes – student moves a token into the last box as the final sound of the word is said.
Write the letters?	• Write the letter; have students trace it. Create the letter with clay. • Discuss the letter features (lines, shape). Trace over the letter with multiple colors.
Know the names of the pictures?	• Tell students the name of the pictures; have students repeat them aloud. • Discuss the words and use each word in context.
Read high-frequency words?	• Create take-home word cards. Use a reward system to track words learned over time. The student uses the word in a sentence, and the teacher writes it down and highlights the high-frequency word. The student re-reads it the next day.

Identify and Name Final Consonant Nn RF.K.3a, RF.K.3c

CCSS: RF.K.3
Know and apply grade-level phonics and word analysis skills in decoding words both in isolation and in text.
a. Demonstrate basic knowledge of one-to-one letter-sound correspondences by producing the primary sound or many of the most frequent sounds for each consonant.
c. Read common high-frequency words by sight.

Lesson Objectives

- Identify and name the letter **Nn.**
- Produce the sound of letter **Nn.**
- Relate the sound /**n**/ to the letter **Nn.**
- Recognize final sound /**n**/ in words/pictures.
- Read common high-frequency words: **like, the.**

Metacognitive Strategy
- Selective Auditory Attention
- Imagery
- Auditory Representation

Academic Language
- letter name, letter sound, initial sound, final sound, ending sound, high-frequency word

Additional Materials
- Sound Spelling Card **Nn**
- Blackline Masters 45, 46

Pre-Assess
Student's ability to recognize the sound represented by the targeted letter of the alphabet and to identify the letter used to represent the corresponding sound in final position.

Introduce

As students participate in this lesson, they will identify the name and sound of the targeted letter and will identify the letter when the sound and name is given orally. Students will apply their knowledge by recognizing the final, or ending, sound of the target letter using pictures. Students apply the skill in context by reading decodable simple sentences that include high-frequency words.

State Learning Goal

Say: *Today we will practice listening to the sound /**n**/ that the letter **n** makes at the end of words.*

Teach

Say: *Letters represent sounds. We remember the sounds each letter makes. We use letters to write words we say. We use letters to read and write words.*

Phonemic Awareness

Show the picture of the sound/spelling card to review the sound.

Say: *Listen to this sound /**n**/. Say it with me: **n**. Say it on your own: **n**.*

Sound-Spelling Correspondence

Show the letter.

Say: *The way we write the sound /**n**/ is with the letter **n**. The letter **n** makes the sound /**n**/.*

Ask: *What is the name of the letter?* (**n**) *What sound does the letter make?* /**n**/

Model

Use BLM 45, Row 1.

Say: *We will look at each picture. Say its name. If we hear the sound /**n**/ at the end of the word, we will circle the picture. If we do not hear the sound /**n**/ at the end, we will cross out the picture.*

Ask: *What do you see in the first picture?* (**man**) *Do you hear the sound /**n**/ at the end of the word **man**?*

Say: *Circle the letter **n**. If you do not hear the sound /**n**/ at the end of the word, then cross out the picture.*

Practice

Use BLM 45, Row 2.

Say: *Look at the picture. Say its name. Write the letter.*

Ask: *What does the second picture show? Do you hear the sound /**n**/ at the end of the word **pin**? Write the letter **n**. Repeat with other words.*

Apply

Blend Words
Use BLM 45, Row 3.

Say: *Look at each letter and listen to the sound as I read.* /**c**/ /**a**/ /**n**/. *Your turn:* /**c**/ /**a**/ /**n**/

Say: *Now we are going to blend the sounds together by stretching them out as we read them.* Point to each letter in a sweeping motion left to right /**caaannn**/.

Ask: *What is the word?* (**can**) Repeat with other words.

High-Frequency words
Use BLM 45, Row 4.

Say: *First, I will point to the word and read it. Then, you will point to the word and we will read it together. Next, I will read a word and you will point to it. Now, you will read the word and I will point to it. Let's write/trace the word as we spell it:* **like**.

Decodable Text
Use BLM 46, Row 1.

Say: *First, I will point to each word as I read the sentence. Then, you will point to each word and we will read together. Next, I will read the sentence and you will point to each word as I read. Now, you will point to each word as you read. Circle all the examples of the letter* **n** *you can find in these sentences. Circle the words* **like** *and* **the** *in the sentences.*

Spelling
Use BLM 46, Row 2.

Say: *Now we can practice writing the sounds we hear in each word. Say one word at a time, stretching each sound. Write a letter for each sound you hear.*

Conclusion

Ask: *What did we learn today? What pictures/words will help you remember the sound* /**n**/ *and the letter* **n** *at the end of a word?*

Say: *We learned that the letter* **n** *makes the sound* /**n**/. *We wrote words using the letter* **n** *at the end.*

Home Connection
Encourage students to practice identifying the final sound /**n**/ and writing the letter **n** with a family member. Encourage students to identify other words that end with letter **n** with their family.

✔ Formative Assessment

If the student completes each task correctly, proceed to the next skill in the sequence. If not, refer to suggested Intervention 2.

Did the student…?	Intervention 2
Identify the names of the letters?	• Use physical rhythmic movements as the letter name is repeated. March while chanting the letter name. Move arms up and down. Sway from side to side.
Identify the sounds of the letters?	• Say words with the target sound in final position, emphasizing the sound. Example: **bunnnn**.
Produce the sounds of the letters?	• Use mirrors to show the movement of the mouth, tongue, and teeth as the sound is produced. • Use hand over mouth to explore movement of air as the sound is produced.
Recognize the final sounds?	• Use Elkonin boxes – student moves a token into the last box as the final sound of the word is said.
Write the letters?	• Write the letter; have students trace it. Create the letter with clay. • Discuss the letter features (lines, shape). Trace over the letter with multiple colors.
Know the names of the pictures?	• Tell students the name of the pictures; have students repeat them aloud. • Discuss the words and use each word in context.
Read high-frequency words?	• Create take-home word cards. Use a reward system to track words learned over time. The student uses the word in a sentence, and the teacher writes it down and highlights the high-frequency word. The student re-reads it the next day.

Identify and Name Final Consonant Pp RF.K.3a, RF.K.3c

CCSS: RF.K.3
Know and apply grade-level phonics and word analysis skills in decoding words both in isolation and in text..
a. Demonstrate basic knowledge of one-to-one letter-sound correspondences by producing the primary sound or many of the most frequent sounds for each consonant.
c. Read common high-frequency words by sight.

Lesson Objectives

- Identify and name the letter **Pp.**
- Produce the sound of letter **Pp.**
- Relate the sound /**p**/ to the letter **Pp.**
- Recognize final sound /**p**/ in words/pictures.
- Read common high-frequency words: **can, go.**

Metacognitive Strategy
- Selective Auditory Attention
- Imagery
- Auditory Representation

Academic Language
- letter name, letter sound, initial sound, final sound, ending sound, high-frequency word

Additional Materials
- Sound Spelling Card **Pp**
- Blackline Masters 47, 48

Pre-Assess
Student's ability to recognize the sound represented by the targeted letter of the alphabet and to identify the letter used to represent the corresponding sound in final position.

Introduce

As students participate in this lesson, they will identify the name and sound of the targeted letter and will identify the letter when the sound and name is given orally. Students will apply their knowledge by recognizing the final, or ending, sound of the target letter using pictures. Students apply the skill in context by reading decodable simple sentences that include high-frequency words.

State Learning Goal

Say: *Today we will practice listening to the sound /**p**/ that the letter **p** makes at the end of words.*

Teach

Say: *Letters represent sounds. We remember the sounds each letter makes. We use letters to write words we say. We use letters to read and write words.*

Phonemic Awareness
Show the picture of the sound/spelling card to review the sound.

Say: *Listen to this sound /**p**/. Say it with me: **p**. Say it on your own: **p**.*

Sound-Spelling Correspondence
Show the letter.

Say: *The way we write the sound /**p**/ is with the letter **p**. The letter **p** makes the sound /**p**/.*

Ask: *What is the name of the letter?* (**p**) *What sound does the letter make?* /**p**/.

Model

Use BLM 47, Row 1.

Say: *We will look at each picture. Say its name. If we hear the sound /**p**/ at the end of the word, we will circle the letter **p**. If we do not hear the sound /**p**/ at the end, we will cross out the letter **p**.*

Ask: *What do you see in the first picture?* (**map**) *Do you hear the sound /**p**/ at the end of the word **map**?*

Say: *Circle the letter **p**. If you do not hear the sound /**p**/ at the end of the word, then cross out the picture.*

Practice

Use BLM 47, Row 2.

Say: *Look at the picture. Say its name. Write the letter.*

Ask: *What does the second picture show? Do you hear the sound /**p**/ at the end of the word **tip**? Write the letter **p**. Repeat with other words.*

Apply

Blend Words

Use BLM 47, Row 3.

Say: *Look at each letter and listen to the sound as I read.* /**s**/ /**i**/ /**p**/. *Your turn:* /**s**/ /**i**/ /**p**/

Say: *Now we are going to blend the sounds together by stretching them out as we read them.* Point to each letter in a sweeping motion left to right /**sssiiip**/.

Ask: *What is the word?* (**sip**) Repeat with other words.

High-Frequency words

Use BLM 47, Row 4.

Say: *First, I will point to the word and read it. Then, you will point to the word and we will read it together. Next, I will read a word and you will point to it. Now, you will read the word and I will point to it. Let's write/trace the word as we spell it:* **can**.

Decodable Text

Use BLM 48, Row 1.

Say: *First, I will point to each word as I read the sentence. Then, you will point to each word and we will read together. Next, I will read the sentence and you will point to each word as I read. Now, you will point to each word as you read. Circle all the examples of the letter* **p** *you can find in these sentences. Circle the words* **can** *and* **go** *in the sentences.*

Spelling

Use BLM 48, Row 2.

Say: *Now we can practice writing the sounds we hear in each word. Say one word at a time, stretching each sound. Write a letter for each sound you hear.*

Conclusion

Ask: *What did we learn today? What pictures/words will help you remember the sound* /**p**/ *and the letter* **p** *at the end of a word?*

Say: *We learned that the letter* **p** *makes the sound* /**p**/. *We wrote words using the letter* **p** *at the end.*

Home Connection

Encourage students to practice identifying the final sound /**p**/ and writing the letter **p** with a family member. Encourage students to identify other words that end with letter **p** with their family.

✔ Formative Assessment

If the student completes each task correctly, proceed to the next skill in the sequence. If not, refer to suggested Intervention 2.

Did the student…?	Intervention 2
Identify the names of the letters?	• Use physical rhythmic movements as the letter name is repeated. March while chanting the letter name. Move arms up and down. Sway from side to side.
Identify the sounds of the letters?	• Say words with the target sound in final position by repeating the words three times. Example: **cap, cap, cap**.
Produce the sounds of the letters?	• Use mirrors to show the movement of the mouth, tongue, and teeth as the sound is produced. • Use hand over mouth to explore movement of air as the sound is produced.
Recognize the final sounds?	• Use Elkonin boxes – student moves a token into the last box as the final sound of the word is said.
Write the letters?	• Write the letter; have students trace it. Create the letter with clay. • Discuss the letter features (lines, shape). Trace over the letter with multiple colors.
Know the names of the pictures?	• Tell students the name of the pictures; have students repeat them aloud. • Discuss the words and use each word in context.
Read high-frequency words?	• Create take-home word cards. Use a reward system to track words learned over time. The student uses the word in a sentence, and the teacher writes it down and highlights the high-frequency word. The student re-reads it the next day.

Identify and Name Final Consonant Bb RF.K.3a, RF.K.3c

CCSS: RF.K.3
Know and apply grade-level phonics and word analysis skills in decoding words both in isolation and in text.
a. Demonstrate basic knowledge of one-to-one letter-sound correspondences by producing the primary sound or many of the most frequent sounds for each consonant.
c. Read common high-frequency words by sight.

Lesson Objectives

- Identify and name the letter **Bb.**
- Produce the sound of letter **Bb.**
- Relate the sound /**b**/ to the letter **Bb.**
- Recognize final sound /**b**/ in words/ pictures.
- Read common high-frequency words: **and, you.**

Metacognitive Strategy
- Selective Auditory Attention
- Imagery
- Auditory Representation

Academic Language
- letter name, letter sound, initial sound, final sound, ending sound, high-frequency word

Additional Materials
- Sound Spelling Card **Bb**
- Blackline Masters 49, 50

Pre-Assess
Student's ability to recognize the sound represented by the targeted letter of the alphabet and to identify the letter used to represent the corresponding sound in final position.

Introduce

As students participate in this lesson, they will identify the name and sound of the targeted letter and will identify the letter when the sound and name is given orally. Students will apply their knowledge by recognizing the final, or ending, sound of the target letter using pictures. Students apply the skill in context by reading decodable simple sentences that include high-frequency words.

State Learning Goal
Say: *Today we will practice listening to the sound /**b**/ that the letter **b** makes at the end of words.*

Teach

Say: *Letters represent sounds. We remember the sounds each letter makes. We use letters to write words we say. We use letters to read and write words.*

Phonemic Awareness
Show the picture of the sound/spelling card to review the sound.

Say: *Listen to this sound /**b**/. Say it with me: **b**. Say it on your own: **b**.*

Sound-Spelling Correspondence
Show the letter.

Say: *The way we write the sound /**b**/ is with the letter **b**. The letter **b** makes the sound /**b**/.*

Ask: *What is the name of the letter? (**b**) What sound does the letter make? /**b**/.*

Model
Use BLM 49, Row 1.

Say: *We will look at each picture. Say its name. If we hear the sound of /**b**/ at the end of the word, we will circle the letter **b**. If we do not hear the sound /**b**/ at the end, we will cross out the picture.*

Ask: *What do you see in the first picture? (**cob**) Do you hear the sound /**b**/ at the end of the word **cob**?*

Say: *Circle the letter **b**. If you do not hear the sound /**b**/ at the end of the word, then cross out the picture.*

Practice
Use BLM 49, Row 2.

Say: *Look at the picture. Say its name. Write the letter.*

Ask: *What does the second picture show? Do you hear the sound /**b**/ at the end of the word **Bob**? Write the letter **b**. Repeat with other words.*

Apply

Blend Words

Use BLM 49, Row 3.

Say: *Look at each letter and listen to the sound as I read.* /s/ /o/ /b/. *Your turn:* /s/ /o/ /b/.

Say: *Now we are going to blend the sounds together by stretching them out as we read them.* Point to each letter in a sweeping motion left to right /**sooob**/.

Ask: *What is the word?* (**sob**) Repeat with other words.

High-Frequency words

Use BLM 49, Row 4.

Say: *First, I will point to the word and read it. Then, you will point to the word and we will read it together. Next, I will read a word and you will point to it. Now, you will read the word and I will point to it. Let's write/trace the word as we spell it:* **and**.

Decodable Text

Use BLM 50, Row 1.

Say: *First, I will point to each word as I read the sentence. Then, you will point to each word and we will read together. Next, I will read the sentence and you will point to each word as I read. Now, you will point to each word as you read. Circle all the examples of the letter* **b** *you can find in these sentences. Circle the words* **and** *and* **you** *in the sentences.*

Spelling

Use BLM 50, Row 2.

Say: *Now we can practice writing the sounds we hear in each word. Say one word at a time, stretching each sound. Write a letter for each sound you hear.*

Conclusion

Ask: *What did we learn today? What pictures/words will help you remember the sound* /**b**/ *and the letter* **b** *at the end of a word?*

Say: *We learned that the letter* **b** *makes the sound* /**b**/. *We wrote words using the letter* **b** *at the end.*

Home Connection

Encourage students to practice identifying the final sound /**b**/ and writing the letter **b** with a family member. Encourage students to identify other words that end with letter **b** with their family.

✔ **Formative Assessment**

If the student completes each task correctly, proceed to the next skill in the sequence. If not, refer to suggested Intervention 2.

Did the student…?	Intervention 2
Identify the names of the letters?	• Use physical rhythmic movements as the letter name is repeated. March while chanting the letter name. Move arms up and down. Sway from side to side.
Identify the sounds of the letters?	• Say words with the target sound in final position by repeating the words three times. Example: **cab, cab, cab**.
Produce the sounds of the letters?	• Use mirrors to show the movement of the mouth, tongue, and teeth as the sound is produced. • Use hand over mouth to explore movement of air as the sound is produced.
Recognize the final sounds?	• Use Elkonin boxes – student moves a token into the last box as the final sound of the word is said.
Write the letters?	• Write the letter; have students trace it. Create the letter with clay. • Discuss the letter features (lines, shape). Trace over the letter with multiple colors.
Know the names of the pictures?	• Tell students the name of the pictures; have students repeat them aloud. • Discuss the words and use each word in context.
Read high-frequency words?	• Create take-home word cards. Use a reward system to track words learned over time. The student uses the word in a sentence, and the teacher writes it down and highlights the high-frequency word. The student re-reads it the next day.

Identify and Name Final Consonant Gg RF.K.3a, RF.K.3c

CCSS: RF.K.3
Know and apply grade-level phonics and word analysis skills in decoding words both in isolation and in text.
a. Demonstrate basic knowledge of one-to-one letter-sound correspondences by producing the primary sound or many of the most frequent sounds for each consonant.
c. Read common high-frequency words by sight.

Lesson Objectives

- Identify and name the letter **Gg.**
- Produce the sound of letter **Gg.**
- Relate the sound /**g**/ to the letter **Gg.**
- Recognize final sound /**g**/ in words/pictures.
- Read common high-frequency words: **jump, one.**

Metacognitive Strategy
- Selective Auditory Attention
- Imagery
- Auditory Representation

Academic Language
- letter name, letter sound, initial sound, final sound, ending sound, high-frequency word

Additional Materials
- Sound Spelling Card **Gg**
- Blackline Masters 51, 52

Pre-Assess
Student's ability to recognize the sound represented by the targeted letter of the alphabet and to identify the letter used to represent the corresponding sound in final position.

Introduce

As students participate in this lesson, they will identify the name and sound of the targeted letter and will identify the letter when the sound and name is given orally. Students will apply their knowledge by recognizing the final, or ending, sound of the target letter using pictures. Students apply the skill in context by reading decodable simple sentences that include high-frequency words.

State Learning Goal

Say: *Today we will practice listening to the sound /**g**/ that the letter **g** makes at the end of words.*

Teach

Say: *Letters represent sounds. We remember the sounds each letter makes. We use letters to write words we say. We use letters to read and write words.*

Phonemic Awareness
Show the picture of the sound/spelling card to review the sound.

Say: *Listen to this sound /**g**/. Say it with me: **g**. Say it on your own: **g**.*

Sound-Spelling Correspondence
Show the letter.

Say: *The way we write the sound /**g**/ is with the letter **g**. The letter **g** makes the sound /**g**/.*

Ask: *What is the name of the letter?* (**g**) *What sound does the letter make?* /**g**/.

Model

Use BLM 51, Row 1.

Say: *We will look at each picture. Say its name. If we hear the sound /**g**/ at the end of the word, we will circle the letter **g**. If we do not hear the sound /**g**/ at the end, we will cross out the picture.*

Ask: *What do you see in the first picture?* (**mug**) *Do you hear the sound /**g**/ at the end of the word **mug**?*

Say: *Circle the letter **g**. If you do not hear the sound /**g**/ at the end of the word, then cross out the picture.*

Practice

Use BLM 51, Row 2.

Say: *Look at the picture. Say its name. Write the letter.*

Ask: *What does the second picture show? Do you hear the sound /**g**/ at the end of the word **rug**? Write the letter **g**. Repeat with other words.*

Apply

Blend Words

Use BLM 51, Row 3.

Say: *Look at each letter and listen to the sound as I read.* /**b**/ /**u**/ /**g**/. *Your turn:* /**b**/ /**u**/ /**g**/.

Say: *Now we are going to blend the sounds together by stretching them out as we read them.* Point to each letter in a sweeping motion left to right /**buuug**/.

Ask: *What is the word?* (**bug**). Repeat with other words.

High-Frequency words

Use BLM 51, Row 4.

Say: *First, I will point to the word and read it. Then, you will point to the word and we will read it together. Next, I will read a word and you will point to it. Now, you will read the word and I will point to it. Let's write/trace the word as we spell it:* **jump**.

Decodable Text

Use BLM 52, Row 1.

Say: *First, I will point to each word as I read the sentence. Then, you will point to each word and we will read together. Next, I will read the sentence and you will point to each word as I read. Now, you will point to each word as you read. Circle all the examples of the letter* **g** *you can find in these sentences. Circle the words* **jump** *and* **one** *in the sentences.*

Spelling

Use BLM 52, Row 2.

Say: *Now we can practice writing the sounds we hear in each word. Say one word at a time, stretching each sound. Write a letter for each sound you hear.*

Conclusion

Ask: *What did we learn today? What pictures/words will help you remember the sound* /**g**/ *and the letter* **g** *at the end of a word?*

Say: *We learned that the letter* **g** *makes the sound* /**g**/. *We wrote words using the letter* **g** *at the end.*

Home Connection

Encourage students to practice identifying the final sound /**g**/ and writing the letter **g** with a family member. Encourage students to identify other words that end with letter **g** with their family.

✔ Formative Assessment

If the student completes each task correctly, proceed to the next skill in the sequence. If not, refer to suggested Intervention 2.

Did the student…?	Intervention 2
Identify the names of the letters?	• Use physical rhythmic movements as the letter name is repeated. March while chanting the letter name. Move arms up and down. Sway from side to side.
Identify the sounds of the letters?	• Say words with the target sound in final position by repeating the words three times. Example: **bag, bag, bag.**
Produce the sounds of the letters?	• Use mirrors to show the movement of the mouth, tongue, and teeth as the sound is produced. • Use hand over mouth to explore movement of air as the sound is produced.
Recognize the final sounds?	• Use Elkonin boxes – student moves a token into the last box as the final sound of the word is said.
Write the letters?	• Write the letter; have students trace it. Create the letter with clay. • Discuss the letter features (lines, shape). Trace over the letter with multiple colors.
Know the names of the pictures?	• Tell students the name of the pictures; have students repeat them aloud. • Discuss the words and use each word in context.
Read high-frequency words?	• Create take-home word cards. Use a reward system to track words learned over time. The student uses the word in a sentence, and the teacher writes it down and highlights the high-frequency word. The student re-reads it the next day.

Identify and Name Final Consonant Dd RF.K.3a, RF.K.3c

CCSS: RF.K.3
Know and apply grade-level phonics and word analysis skills in decoding words both in isolation and in text.
a. Demonstrate basic knowledge of one-to-one letter-sound correspondences by producing the primary sound or many of the most frequent sounds for each consonant.
c. Read common high-frequency words by sight.

Lesson Objectives

- Identify and name the letter **Dd.**
- Produce the sound of letter **Dd.**
- Relate the sound /**d**/ to the letter **Dd.**
- Recognize final sound /**d**/ in words/pictures.
- Read common high-frequency words: **no, and.**

Metacognitive Strategy
- Selective Auditory Attention
- Imagery
- Auditory Representation

Academic Language
- letter name, letter sound, initial sound, final sound, ending sound, high-frequency word

Additional Materials
- Sound Spelling Card **Dd**
- Blackline Masters 53, 54

Pre-Assess
Student's ability to recognize the sound represented by the targeted letter of the alphabet and to identify the letter used to represent the corresponding sound in final position.

Introduce

As students participate in this lesson, they will identify the name and sound of the targeted letter and will identify the letter when the sound and name is given orally. Students will apply their knowledge by recognizing the final, or ending, sound of the target letter using pictures. Students apply the skill in context by reading decodable simple sentences that include high-frequency words.

State Learning Goal

Say: *Today we will practice listening to the sound /**d**/ that the letter **d** makes at the end of words.*

Teach

Say: *Letters represent sounds. We remember the sounds each letter makes. We use letters to write words we say. We use letters to read and write words.*

Phonemic Awareness
Show the picture of the sound/spelling card to review the sound.

Say: *Listen to this sound /**d**/. Say it with me: **d**. Say it on your own: **d**.*

Sound-Spelling Correspondence
Show the letter.

Say: *The way we write the sound /**d**/ is with the letter **d**. The letter **d** makes the sound /**d**/.*

Ask: *What is the name of the letter? (**d**) What sound does the letter make? /**d**/.*

Model

Use BLM 53, Row 1.

Say: *We will look at each picture. Say its name. If we hear the sound /**d**/ at the end of the word, we will circle the letter **d**. If we do not hear the sound /**d**/ at the end, we will cross out the picture.*

Ask: *What do you see in the first picture? (**bed**) Do you hear the sound /**d**/ at the end of the word **bed**?*

Say: *Circle the letter **d**. If you do not hear the sound /**d**/ at the end of the word, then cross out the picture.*

Practice

Use BLM 53, Row 2.

Say: *Look at the picture. Say its name. Write the letter.*

Ask: *What does the second picture show? Do you hear the sound /**d**/ at the end of the word **sad**? Write the letter **d**. Repeat with other words.*

Apply

Blend Words
Use BLM 53, Row 3.

Say: *Look at each letter and listen to the sound as I read. /k/ /i/ /d/. Your turn:* /k/ /i/ /d/.

Say: *Now we are going to blend the sounds together by stretching them out as we read them.* Point to each letter in a sweeping motion left to right /**kiiid**/.

Ask: *What is the word?* (**kid**) Repeat with other words.

High-Frequency words
Use BLM 53, Row 4.

Say: *First, I will point to the word and read it. Then, you will point to the word and we will read it together. Next, I will read a word and you will point to it. Now, you will read the word and I will point to it. Let's write/trace the word as we spell it:* **no**.

Decodable Text
Use BLM 54, Row 1.

Say: *First, I will point to each word as I read the sentence. Then, you will point to each word and we will read together. Next, I will read the sentence and you will point to each word as I read. Now, you will point to each word as you read. Circle all the examples of the letter* **d** *you can find in these sentences. Circle the words* **no** *and* **and** *in the sentences.*

Spelling
Use BLM 54, Row 2.

Say: *Now we can practice writing the sounds we hear in each word. Say one word at a time, stretching each sound. Write a letter for each sound you hear.*

Conclusion

Ask: *What did we learn today? What pictures/words will help you remember the sound /d/ and the letter* **d** *at the end of a word?*

Say: *We learned that the letter* **d** *makes the sound /d/. We wrote words using the letter* **d** *at the end.*

Home Connection
Encourage students to practice identifying the final sound /**d**/ and writing the letter **d** with a family member. Encourage students to identify other words that end with letter **d** with their family.

✔ Formative Assessment

If the student completes each task correctly, proceed to the next skill in the sequence. If not, refer to suggested Intervention 2.

Did the student…?	Intervention 2
Identify the names of the letters?	• Use physical rhythmic movements as the letter name is repeated. March while chanting the letter name. Move arms up and down. Sway from side to side.
Identify the sounds of the letters?	• Say words with the target sound in final position by repeating the words three times. Example: **dad, dad, dad**.
Produce the sounds of the letters?	• Use mirrors to show the movement of the mouth, tongue, and teeth as the sound is produced. • Use hand over mouth to explore movement of air as the sound is produced.
Recognize the final sounds?	• Use Elkonin boxes – student moves a token into the last box as the final sound of the word is said.
Write the letters?	• Write the letter; have students trace it. Create the letter with clay. • Discuss the letter features (lines, shape). Trace over the letter with multiple colors.
Know the names of the pictures?	• Tell students the name of the pictures; have students repeat them aloud. • Discuss the words and use each word in context.
Read high-frequency words?	• Create take-home word cards. Use a reward system to track words learned over time. The student uses the word in a sentence, and the teacher writes it down and highlights the high-frequency word. The student re-reads it the next day.

Identify and Name Final Consonant Xx RF.K.3a, RF.K.3c

CCSS: RF.K.3
Know and apply grade-level phonics and word analysis skills in decoding words both in isolation and in text.
a. Demonstrate basic knowledge of one-to-one letter-sound correspondences by producing the primary sound or many of the most frequent sounds for each consonant.
c. Read common high-frequency words by sight.

Lesson Objectives

- Identify and name the letter **Xx.**
- Produce the sound of letter **Xx.**
- Relate the sound **/x/** to the letter **Xx.**
- Recognize final sound **/x/** in words/pictures.
- Read common high-frequency words: **to, my.**

Metacognitive Strategy
- Selective Auditory Attention
- Imagery
- Auditory Representation

Academic Language
- letter name, letter sound, initial sound, final sound, ending sound, high-frequency word

Additional Materials
- Sound Spelling Card **Xx**
- Blackline Masters 55, 56

Pre-Assess
Student's ability to recognize the sound represented by the targeted letter of the alphabet and to identify the letter used to represent the corresponding sound in final position.

Introduce

As students participate in this lesson, they will identify the name and sound of the targeted letter and will identify the letter when the sound and name is given orally. Students will apply their knowledge by recognizing the final, or ending, sound of the target letter using pictures. Students apply the skill in context by reading decodable simple sentences that include high-frequency words.

State Learning Goal

Say: *Today we will practice listening to the sound /x/ that the letter x makes at the end of words.*

Teach

Say: *Letters represent sounds. We remember the sounds each letter makes. We use letters to write words we say. We use letters to read and write words.*

Phonemic Awareness

Show the picture of the sound/spelling card to review the sound.

Say: *Listen to this sound /x/. Say it with me: (x) Say it on your own: x.*

Sound-Spelling Correspondence

Show the letter.

Say: *The way we write the sound. /x/ is with the letter x. The letter x makes the sound /x/.*

Ask: *What is the name of the letter? (x) What sound does the letter make? /x/*

Model

Use BLM 55, Row 1.

Say: *We will look at each picture. Say its name. If we hear the sound /x/ at the end of the word, we will circle the letter x. If we do not hear the sound /x/ at the end, we will cross out the picture.*

Ask: *What do you see in the first picture? (fox) Do you hear the sound /x/ at the end of the word fox?*

Say: *Circle the letter x. If you do not hear the sound /x/ at the end of the word, then cross out the picture.*

Practice

Use BLM 55, Row 2.

Say: *Look at the picture. Say its name. Write the letter.*

Ask: *What does the second picture show? Do you hear the sound /x/ at the end of the word ox? Write the letter x. Repeat with other words.*

Apply

Blend Words

Use BLM 55, Row 3.

Say: *Look at each letter and listen to the sound as I read. /M/ /a/ /x/. Your turn: /M/ /a/ /x/.*

Say: *Now we are going to blend the sounds together by stretching them out as we read them.* Point to each letter in a sweeping motion left to right /**mmmaaax**/.

Ask: *What is the word?* (**Max**) Repeat with other words.

High-Frequency words

Use BLM 55, Row 4.

Say: *First, I will point to the word and read it. Then, you will point to the word and we will read it together. Next, I will read a word and you will point to it. Now, you will read the word and I will point to it. Let's write/trace the word as we spell it:* **to**.

Decodable Text

Use BLM 56, Row 1.

Say: *First, I will point to each word as I read the sentence. Then, you will point to each word and we will read together. Next, I will read the sentence and you will point to each word as I read. Now, you will point to each word as you read. Circle all the examples of the letter* **x** *you can find in these sentences. Circle the words* **to** *and* **my** *in the sentences.*

Spelling

Use BLM 56, Row 2.

Say: *Now we can practice writing the sounds we hear in each word. Say one word at a time, stretching each sound. Write a letter for each sound you hear.*

Conclusion

Ask: *What did we learn today? What pictures/words will help you remember the sound /x/ and the letter x at the end of a word?*

Say: *We learned that the letter* **x** *makes the sound /x/. We wrote words using the letter* **x** *at the end.*

Home Connection

Encourage students to practice identifying the final sound /**x**/ and writing the letter **x** with a family member. Encourage students to identify other words that end with letter **x** with their family.

✔ Formative Assessment

If the student completes each task correctly, proceed to the next skill in the sequence. If not, refer to suggested Intervention 2.

Did the student…?	Intervention 2
Identify the names of the letters?	• Use physical rhythmic movements as the letter name is repeated. March while chanting the letter name. Move arms up and down. Sway from side to side.
Identify the sounds of the letters?	• Say words with the target sound in final position by repeating the words three times. Example: **fox, fox, fox.**
Produce the sounds of the letters?	• Use mirrors to show the movement of the mouth, tongue, and teeth as the sound is produced. • Use hand over mouth to explore movement of air as the sound is produced.
Recognize the final sounds?	• Use Elkonin boxes – student moves a token into the last box as the final sound of the word is said.
Write the letters?	• Write the letter; have students trace it. Create the letter with clay. • Discuss the letter features (lines, shape). Trace over the letter with multiple colors.
Know the names of the pictures?	• Tell students the name of the pictures; have students repeat them aloud. • Discuss the words and use each word in context.
Read high-frequency words?	• Create take-home word cards. Use a reward system to track words learned over time. The student uses the word in a sentence, and the teacher writes it down and highlights the high-frequency word. The student re-reads it the next day.

Identify and Name Initial Short Vowel a   RF.K.3b, RF.K.3c

CCSS: RF.K.3
Know and apply grade-level phonics and word analysis skills in decoding words both in isolation and in text.
b. Associate the long and short sounds with common spellings (graphemes) for the five major vowels.
c. Read common high-frequency words by sight.

Lesson Objectives

- Identify and name the letter **Aa**.
- Produce the sound of letter **Aa**.
- Relate the sound /a/ to the letter **Aa**.
- Recognize **initial short vowel** sound /a/ in words/pictures.
- Read common high-frequency words: **I, like**.

Metacognitive Strategy
- Selective Auditory Attention
- Imagery
- Auditory Representation

Academic Language
- letter name, letter sound, initial sound, vowel, short vowel sound long vowel sound

Additional Materials
- Sound Spelling Card **Aa**
- Blackline Masters 57, 58

Pre-Assess
Student's ability to recognize the sound represented by the target letter of the alphabet and to identify the letter used to represent the corresponding sound.

Introduce

As students participate in this lesson, they will identify the name and sound of the target letter and will identify the letter when the sound and name is given orally. Students will apply their knowledge by recognizing the short sound of the target letter using pictures. Students apply the skill in context by reading simple decodable sentences that include high-frequency words.

State Learning Goal

Say: *The letter **a** is a vowel. It has two sounds. The long sound /ā/ and the short sound /a/. Today we will listen to the short sound of the letter **a** at the beginning of words.*

Teach

Say: *Letters represent sounds. We remember the sounds each letter makes. We use letters to write words we say. We use letters to read and write words.*

Phonemic Awareness

Show the picture of the sound/spelling card to review sounds.

Say: *Listen to this sound: /a/. Say it with me: /a/. Say it on your own: /a/.*

Sound-Spelling Correspondence

Show the letter.

Say: *The way we write the sound /a/ is with the letter **a**. The letter **a** makes the sound /a/.*

Ask: *What is the name of the letter? (**a**) What sound does the letter make? /a/.*

Model

Use BLM 57, Row 1.

Say: *We will look at each picture. Say its name. If we hear the sound of /a/ at the beginning of the word, we will circle the picture. If we do not hear the sound /a/ at the beginning, we will cross out the picture.*

Ask: *What does the first picture show? (**apple**) Do you hear the sound /a/ at the beginning of **apple?***

Say: *If you do not hear the sound /a/ at the beginning of the word, then cross out the picture.*

Practice

Use BLM 57, Row 2.

Say: *Look at the picture. Say its name. Write the letter.*

Ask: *What does the third picture show? (**ax**) Do you hear the sound /a/ at the beginning of the word **ax**? Write the letter **a**. Repeat with other words.*

Apply

Blend Words
Use BLM 57, Row 3

Say: *Look at each letter and listen to the sound as I read:* /**a**/ /**n**/ /**t**/. *Your turn:* /**a**/ /**n**/ /**t**/

Say: *Now we are going to blend the sounds together by stretching them out as we read them.* Point to each letter in a sweeping motion left to right /**aaannnt**/.

Ask: *What is the word?* (**ant**). Repeat with other words.

High-Frequency words
Use BLM 57, Row 4.

Say: *First, I will point to the word and read it. Then, you will point to the word and we will read it together. Next, I will read a word and you will point to it. Now, you will read the word and I will point to it. Let's write/trace the word as we spell it:* **I.**

Decodable Text
Use BLM 58, Row 1.

Say: *First, I will point to each word as I read the sentence. Then, you will point to each word and we will read together. Next, I will read the sentence and you will point to each word as I read. Now, you will point to each word as you read. Circle all the examples of the letter* **a** *you can find in these sentences. Circle the word* **I** *and* **like** *in the sentences.*

Spelling
Use BLM 58, Row 2.

Say: *Now we can practice writing the sounds we hear in each word. Say one word at a time, stretching each sound. Write a letter for each sound you hear.*

Conclusion
Ask: *What did we learn today? What pictures/words will help you remember the sound* /**a**/ *and the letter* **a**?

Say: *We learned that the letter* **a** *makes the sound* /**a**/ *at the beginning of some words.*

Home Connection
Encourage students to practice identifying initial short vowel sound **a** and writing the letter **a** with a family member. Encourage students to identify other words that begin with the short vowel sound **a** with their family.

✔ Formative Assessment

If the student completes each task correctly, proceed to the next skill in the sequence. If not, refer to suggested intervention 2.

Did the student…?	Intervention 2
Identify the names of the letters?	• Use physical rhythmic movements as the letter name is repeated. March while chanting the letter name. Move arms up and down. Sway from side to side.
Identify the sounds of the letters?	• Use chants that repeat the sound several times, ending with a word that begins with the sound. Example: /a/ /a/ /a/ **apple.**
Produce the sounds of the letters?	• Use mirrors to show the movement of mouth, tongue, teeth as the sound is produced.
Recognize the beginning sounds?	• Use Elkonin boxes – student moves a token into the first box as the beginning sound of the word is said.
Write the letters?	• Write the letter; have students trace it. Create the letter with clay.
Know the names of the pictures?	• Tell students the name of the picture, have students repeat it aloud.
Read high-frequency words?	• Create take-home word cards. Use a reward system to track words learned over time. The student uses the word in a sentence, and the teacher writes it down and highlights the high-frequency word. The student re-reads it the next day.

Identify and Name Initial Short Vowel i RF.K.3b, RF.K.3c

CCSS: RF.K.3
Know and apply grade-level phonics and word analysis skills in decoding words both in isolation and in text.
b. Associate the long and short sounds with common spellings (graphemes) for the five major vowels.
c. Read common high-frequency words by sight.

Lesson Objectives

- Identify and name the letter **i.**
- Produce the sound of the letter **i.**
- Relate the sound **/i/** to the letter **i.**
- Recognize **initial short vowel** sound **/i/** in words/pictures.
- Read common high-frequency words: **she, can**

Metacognitive Strategy
- Selective Auditory Attention
- Imagery
- Auditory Representation

Academic Language
- letter name, letter sound, initial sound, vowel, short vowel sound long vowel sound

Additional Materials
- Sound Spelling Card **Ii**
- Blackline Masters 59, 60

Pre-Assess
Student's ability to recognize the sound represented by the target letter of the alphabet and to identify the letter used to represent the corresponding sound.

Introduce

As students participate in this lesson, they will identify the name and sound of the target letter and will identify the letter when the sound and name is given orally. Students will apply their knowledge by recognizing the short sound of the target letter using pictures. Students apply the skill in context by reading simple decodable sentences that include high-frequency words.

State Learning Goal

Say: *The letter* **i** *is a vowel. It has two sounds. The long sound /ī/ and the short sound /ĭ/. Today we will listen to the short sound of the letter* **i** *at the beginning of words.*

Teach

Say: *Letters represent sounds. We remember the sounds each letter makes. We use letters to write words we say. We use letters to read and write words.*

Phonemic Awareness

Show the picture of the sound/spelling card to review sounds.

Say: *Listen to this sound: /ĭ/. Say it with me: /ĭ/. Say it on your own: /ĭ/.*

Sound-Spelling Correspondence

Show the letter.

Say: *The way we write the sound /ĭ/ is with the letter* **i**. *The letter* **i** *makes the sound /ĭ/.*

Ask: *What is the name of the letter?* (**i**) *What sound does the letter make?* /ĭ/.

Model

Use BLM 59, Row 1.

Say: *We will look at each picture. Say its name. If we hear the sound /ĭ/ at the beginning of the word, we will circle the picture. If we do not hear the sound /ĭ/ at the beginning, we will cross out the picture.*

Ask: *What does the first picture show?* (**ink**) *Do you hear the sound /ĭ/ at the beginning of* **ink**?

Say: *If you do not hear the sound /ĭ/ at the beginning of the word, then cross out the picture.*

Practice

Use BLM 59, Row 2.

Say: *Look at the picture. Say its name. Write the letter.*

Say: *What does the second picture show?* (**ill**) *Do you hear the sound /ĭ/ at the beginning of the word* **ill**? *Write the letter* **i**. *Repeat with other words.*

Apply

Blend Words
Use BLM 59, Row 3

Say: *Look at each letter and listen to the sound as I read:* /**i**/ /**n**/. *Your turn:* /**i**/ /**n**/.

Say: *Now we are going to blend the sounds together by stretching them out as we read them.* Point to each letter in a sweeping motion left to right /**iiinnn**/.

Ask: *What is the word?* (**in**) Repeat with other words.

High-Frequency words
Use BLM 59, Row 4.

Say: *First, I will point to the word and read it. Then, you will point to the word and we will read it together. Next, I will read a word and you will point to it. Now, you will read the word and I will point to it. Let's write/trace the word as we spell it:* **she.**

Decodable Text
Use BLM 60, Row 1.

Say: *First, I will point to each word as I read the sentence. Then, you will point to each word and we will read together. Next, I will read the sentence and you will point to each word as I read. Now, you will point to each word as you read. Circle all the examples of the letter* **i** *you can find in these sentences. Circle the words* **she** *and* **can** *in the sentences.*

Spelling
Use BLM 60, Row 2.

Say: *Now we can practice writing the sounds we hear in each word. Say one word at a time, stretching each sound. Write a letter for each sound you hear.*

Conclusion

Ask: *What did we learn today? What pictures/words will help you remember the sound* /**i**/ *and the letter* **i**?

Say: *We learned that the letter* **i** *makes the sound* /**i**/ *at the beginning of some words.*

Home Connection
Encourage students to practice identifying initial short vowel sound **i** and writing the letter **i** with a family member. Encourage students to identify other words that begin with the short vowel sound **i** with their family.

✔ Formative Assessment

If the student completes each task correctly, proceed to the next skill in the sequence. If not, refer to suggested intervention 2.

Did the student...?	Intervention 2
Identify the names of the letters?	• Use physical rhythmic movements as the letter name is repeated. March while chanting the letter name. Move arms up and down. Sway from side to side.
Identify the sounds of the letters?	• Use chants that repeat the sound several times, ending with a word that begins with the sound. Example: /i/ /i/ /i/ **ink.**
Produce the sounds of the letters?	• Use mirrors to show the movement of mouth, tongue, teeth as the sound is produced. Use hand over mouth to explore movement of air as the sound is produced.
Recognize the beginning sounds?	• Use Elkonin boxes – student moves a token into the first box as the beginning sound of the word is said.
Write the letters?	• Write the letter; have students trace it. Create the letter with clay.
Know the names of the pictures?	• Tell students the name of the picture, have students repeat it aloud.
Read high-frequency words?	• Create take-home word cards. Use a reward system to track words learned over time. The student uses the word in a sentence, and the teacher writes it down and highlights the high-frequency word. The student re-reads it the next day.

Identify and Name Initial Short Vowel o RF.K.3b, RF.K.3c

CCSS: RF.K.3
Know and apply grade-level phonics and word analysis skills in decoding words both in isolation and in text.
b. Associate the long and short sounds with common spellings (graphemes) for the five major vowels.
c. Read common high-frequency words by sight.

Lesson Objectives

- Identify and name the letter **Oo.**
- Produce the sound of letter **Oo.**
- Relate the sound /**o**/ to the letter **Oo.**
- Recognize **initial short vowel** sound /**o**/ in words/pictures.
- Read common high-frequency words: **he, has.**

Metacognitive Strategy
- Selective Auditory Attention
- Imagery
- Auditory Representation

Academic Language
- letter name, letter sound, initial sound, vowel, short vowel sound long vowel sound

Additional Materials
- Sound Spelling Card **Oo**
- Blackline Masters 61, 62

Pre-Assess
Student's ability to recognize the sound represented by the target letter of the alphabet and to identify the letter used to represent the corresponding sound.

Introduce

As students participate in this lesson, they will identify the name and sound of the target letter and will identify the letter when the sound and name is given orally. Students will apply their knowledge by recognizing the short sound of the target letter using pictures. Students apply the skill in context by reading simple decodable sentences that include high-frequency words.

State Learning Goal
Say: *The letter* **o** *is a vowel. It has two sounds. The long sound /ō/ and the short sound /o/. Today we will listen to the short sound of the letter* **o** *at the beginning of words.*

Teach
Say: *Letters represent sounds. We remember the sounds each letter makes. We use letters to write words we say. We use letters to read and write words.*

Phonemic Awareness
Show the picture of the sound/spelling card to review sounds.

Say: *Listen to this sound: /o/. Say it with me: /o/. Say it on your own: /o/.*

Sound-Spelling Correspondence
Show the letter.

Say: *The way we write the sound /o/ is with the letter* **o***. The letter* **o** *makes the sound /o/.*

Ask: *What is the name of the letter?* (**o**) *What sound does the letter make?* /**o**/.

Model
Use BLM 61, Row 1.

Say: *We will look at each picture. Say its name. If we hear the sound /o/ at the beginning of the word, we will circle the picture. If we do not hear the sound /o/ at the beginning, we will cross out the picture.*

Ask: *What does the first picture show?* (**ox**) *Do you hear the sound /o/ at the beginning of* **ox***?*

Say: *If you do not hear the sound /o/ at the beginning of the word, then cross out the picture.*

Practice
Use BLM 61, Row 2.

Say: *Look at the picture. Say its name. Write the letter.*

Ask: *What does the second picture show?* (**on**) *Do you hear the sound /o/ at the beginning of the word* **on***? Write the letter* **o***.* Repeat with other words.

Apply

Blend Words
Use BLM 61, Row 3

Say: *Look at each letter and listen to the sound as I read:* /**o**/ /**f**/ /**f**/. *Your turn:* /**o**/ /**f**/ /**f**/.

Say: *Now we are going to blend the sounds together by stretching them out as we read them.* Point to each letter in a sweeping motion left to right /**ooofff**/.

Ask: *What is the word?* (**off**) Repeat with other words.

High-Frequency words
Use BLM 61, Row 4.

Say: *First, I will point to the word and read it. Then, you will point to the word and we will read it together. Next, I will read a word and you will point to it. Now, you will read the word and I will point to it. Let's write/trace the word as we spell it:* **he.**

Decodable Text
Use BLM 62, Row 1.

Say: *First, I will point to each word as I read the sentence. Then, you will point to each word and we will read together. Next, I will read the sentence and you will point to each word as I read. Now, you will point to each word as you read. Circle all the examples of the letter* **o** *you can find in these sentences. Circle the words* **he** *and* **has** *in the sentences.*

Spelling
Use BLM 62, Row 1.

Say: *Now we can practice writing the sounds we hear in each word. Say one word at a time, stretching each sound. Write a letter for each sound you hear.*

Conclusion

Ask: *What did we learn today? What pictures/words will help you remember the sound* /**o**/ *and the letter* **o**?

Say: *We learned that the letter* **o** *makes the sound* /**o**/ *at the beginning of some words.*

Home Connection
Encourage students to practice identifying initial short vowel sound **o** and writing the letter **o** with a family member. Encourage students to identify other words that begin with the short vowel sound **o** with their family.

✔ Formative Assessment

If the student completes each task correctly, proceed to the next skill in the sequence. If not, refer to suggested intervention 2.

Did the student…?	Intervention 2
Identify the names of the letters?	• Use physical rhythmic movements as the letter name is repeated. March while chanting the letter name. Move arms up and down. Sway from side to side.
Identify the sounds of the letters?	• Use chants that repeat the sound several times, ending with a word that begins with sound. Example: /**o**/ /**o**/ /**o**/ **ox.**
Produce the sounds of the letters?	• Use mirrors to show the movement of mouth, tongue, teeth as the sound is produced.
Recognize the beginning sounds?	• Use Elkonin boxes – student moves a token into the first box as the beginning sound of the word is said.
Write the letters?	• Write the letter; have students trace it. Create the letter with clay.
Know the names of the pictures?	• Tell students the name of the picture, have students repeat it aloud.
Read high-frequency words?	• Create take-home word cards. Use a reward system to track words learned over time. The student uses the word in a sentence, and the teacher writes it down and highlights the high-frequency word. The student re-reads it the next day.

Identify and Name Initial Short Vowel u RF.K.3b, RF.K.3c

CCSS: RF.K.3
Know and apply grade-level phonics and word analysis skills in decoding words both in isolation and in text.
b. Associate the long and short sounds with common spellings (graphemes) for the five major vowels.
c. Read common high-frequency words by sight.

Lesson Objectives

- Identify and name the letter **Uu**.
- Produce the sound of letter **Uu**.
- Relate the sound /**o**/ to the letter **Uu**.
- Recognize **initial short vowel** sound /**u**/ in words/pictures.
- Read common high-frequency words: **with, big.**

Metacognitive Strategy
- Selective Auditory Attention
- Imagery
- Auditory Representation

Academic Language
- letter name, letter sound, initial sound, vowel, short vowel sound long vowel sound

Additional Materials
- Sound Spelling Card **Uu**
- Blackline Masters 63, 64

Pre-Assess
Student's ability to recognize the sound represented by the target letter of the alphabet and to identify the letter used to represent the corresponding sound.

Introduce

As students participate in this lesson, they will identify the name and sound of the target letter and will identify the letter when the sound and name is given orally. Students will apply their knowledge by recognizing the short sound of the target letter using pictures. Students apply the skill in context by reading simple decodable sentences that include high-frequency words.

State Learning Goal

Say: *The letter **u** is a vowel. It has two sounds. The long sound /ū/ and the short sound /**u**/. Today we will listen to the short sound of the letter **u** at the beginning of words.*

Teach

Say: *Letters represent sounds. We remember the sounds each letter makes. We use letters to write words we say. We use letters to read and write words.*

Phonemic Awareness

Show the picture of the sound/spelling card to review sounds.

Say: *Listen to this sound: /**u**/. Say it with me: /**u**/. Say it on your own: /**u**/.*

Sound-Spelling Correspondence

Show the letter.

Say: *The way we write the sound /**u**/ is with the letter **u**. The letter **u** makes the sound /**u**/.*

Ask: *What is the name of the letter? (**u**) What sound does the letter make? /**u**/.*

Model

Use BLM 63, Row 1.

Say: *We will look at each picture. Say its name. If we hear the sound /**u**/ at the beginning of the word, we will circle the picture. If we do not hear the sound /**u**/ at the beginning, we will cross out the picture.*

Ask: *What does the picture show? (**up**) Do you hear the sound /**u**/ at the beginning of **up**?*

Say: *If you do not hear the sound /**u**/ at the beginning of the word, then cross out the picture.*

Practice

Use BLM 63, Row 2.

Say: *Look at the picture. Say its name. Write the letter.*

Ask: *What does the second picture show? (**under**) Do you hear the sound /**u**/ at the beginning of the word **under**? Write the letter **u**. Repeat with other words.*

Apply

Blend Words

Use BLM 63, Row 3

Say: *Look at each letter and listen to the sound as I read: /u/ /m/ /b/ /r/ /e/ /l/ /l/ /a/. Your turn:*

Say: *Now we are going to blend the sounds together by stretching them out as we read them.*

Point to each letter in a sweeping motion left to right /**uuummmbrrreeelllaaa**/.

Ask: *What is the word?* (**umbrella**) Repeat with other words.

High-Frequency words

Use BLM 63, Row 4.

Say: *First, I will point to the word and read it. Then, you will point to the word and we will read it together. Next, I will read a word and you will point to it. Now, you will read the word and I will point to it. Let's write/trace the word as we spell it:* **with.**

Decodable Text

Use BLM 64, Row 1.

Say: *First, I will point to each word as I read the sentence. Then, you will point to each word and we will read together. Next, I will read the sentence and you will point to each word as I read. Now, you will point to each word as you read. Circle all the examples of the letter* **u** *you can find in these sentences. Circle the words* **with** *and* **big** *in the sentences.*

Spelling

Use BLM 64, Row 2.

Say: *Now we can practice writing the sounds we hear in each word. Say one word at a time, stretching each sound. Write a letter for each sound you hear.*

Conclusion

Ask: *What did we learn today? What pictures/words will help you remember the sound /u/ and the letter* **u***?*

Say: *We learned that the letter* **u** *makes the sound /u/ at the beginning of some words.*

Home Connection

Encourage students to practice identifying initial short vowel sound **u** and writing the letter **u** with a family member. Encourage students to identify other words that begin with the short vowel sound **u** with their family.

✔ Formative Assessment

If the student completes each task correctly, proceed to the next skill in the sequence. If not, refer to suggested intervention 2.

Did the student…?	Intervention 2
Identify the names of the letters?	• Use physical rhythmic movements as the letter name is repeated. March while chanting the letter name. Move arms up and down. Sway from side to side.
Identify the sounds of the letters?	• Use alliteration, chants that repeat the sound several times and followed by a word that begins with the sound. Example: /u/ /u/ /u/ **up**.
Produce the sounds of the letters?	• Use mirrors to show the movement of mouth, tongue, teeth as the sound is produced.
Recognize the beginning sounds?	• Use Elkonin boxes – student moves a token into the first box as the beginning sound of the word is said.
Write the letters?	• Write the letter; have students trace it. Create the letter with clay.
Know the names of the pictures?	• Tell students the name of the picture, have students repeat it aloud.
Read high-frequency words?	• Create take-home word cards. Use a reward system to track words learned over time. The student uses the word in a sentence, and the teacher writes it down and highlights the high-frequency word. The student re-reads it the next day.

Identify and Name Initial Short Vowel e RF.K.3b, RF.K.3c

CCSS: RF.K.3
Know and apply grade-level phonics and word analysis skills in decoding words both in isolation and in text.
b. Associate the long and short sounds with common spellings (graphemes) for the five major vowels.
c. Read common high-frequency words by sight.

Lesson Objectives

- Identify and name the letter **Ee**.
- Produce the sound of letter **Ee**.
- Relate the sound /**e**/ to the letter **Ee**.
- Recognize **initial short vowel** sound /**e**/ in words/pictures.
- Read common high-frequency words: **for, no.**

Metacognitive Strategy
- Selective Auditory Attention
- Imagery
- Auditory Representation

Academic Language
- letter name, letter sound, initial sound, vowel, short vowel sound long vowel sound

Additional Materials
- Sound Spelling Card **Ee**
- Blackline Masters 65, 66

Pre-Assess
Student's ability to recognize the sound represented by the target letter of the alphabet and to identify the letter used to represent the corresponding sound.

Introduce

As students participate in this lesson, they will identify the name and sound of the target letter and will identify the letter when the sound and name is given orally. Students will apply their knowledge by recognizing the short sound of the target letter using pictures. Students apply the skill in context by reading simple decodable sentences that include high-frequency words.

State Learning Goal

Say: *The letter **e** is a vowel. It has two sounds. The long sound /ē/ and the short sound /**e**/. Today we will listen to the short sound of the letter **e** at the beginning of words.*

Teach

Say: *Letters represent sounds. We remember the sounds each letter makes. We use letters to write words we say. We use letters to read and write words.*

Phonemic Awareness

Show the picture of the sound/spelling card to review sounds.

Say: *Listen to this sound: /**e**/. Say it with me: /**e**/. Say it on your own: /**e**/.*

Sound-Spelling Correspondence

Show the letter.

Say: *The way we write the sound /**e**/ is with the letter **e**. The letter **e** makes the sound /**e**/.*

Ask: *What is the name of the letter?* (**e**) *What sound does the letter make?* /**e**/.

Model

Use BLM 65, Row 1.

Say: *We will look at each picture. Say its name. If we hear the sound /**e**/ at the beginning of the word, we will circle the picture. If we do not hear the sound /**e**/ at the beginning, we will cross out the picture.*

Ask: *What does the first picture show?* (**egg**) *Do you hear the sound /**e**/ at the beginning of **egg**?*

Say: *If you do not hear the sound /**e**/ at the beginning of the word, then cross out the picture.*

Practice

Use BLM 65, Row 2.

Say: *Look at the picture. Say its name. Write the letter.*

Ask: *What does the second picture show?* (**elf**) *Do you hear the sound /**e**/ at the beginning of the word **elf**? Write the letter **e**. Repeat with other words.*

Apply

Blend Words
Use BLM 65, Row 3

Say: *Look at each letter and listen to the sound as I read: /e/ /n/ /d/. Your turn: /e/ /n/ /d/.*

Say: *Now we are going to blend the sounds together by stretching them out as we read them.* Point to each letter in a sweeping motion left to right /**eeennnd**/.

Ask: *What is the word?* (**end**) Repeat with other words.

High-Frequency words
Use BLM 65, Row 4.

Say: *First, I will point to the word and read it. Then, you will point to the word and we will read it together. Next, I will read a word and you will point to it. Now, you will read the word and I will point to it. Let's write/trace the word as we spell it:* **for.**

Decodable Text
Use BLM 66, Row 1.

Say: *First, I will point to each word as I read the sentence. Then, you will point to each word and we will read together. Next, I will read the sentence and you will point to each word as I read. Now, you will point to each word as you read. Circle all the examples of the letter* **e** *you can find in these sentences. Circle the words* **for** *and* **no** *in the sentences.*

Spelling
Use BLM 66, Row 2.

Say: *Now we can practice writing the sounds we hear in each word. Say one word at a time, stretching each sound. Write a letter for each sound you hear.*

Conclusion

Ask: *What did we learn today? What pictures/words will help you remember the sound /e/ and the letter* **e**?

Say: *We learned that the letter* **e** *makes the sound /e/ at the beginning of some words.*

Home Connection
Encourage students to practice identifying initial short vowel sound **e** and writing the letter **e** with a family member. Encourage students to identify other words that begin with the short vowel sound **e** with their family.

✔ Formative Assessment

If the student completes each task correctly, proceed to the next skill in the sequence. If not, refer to suggested intervention 2.

Did the student…?	Intervention 2
Identify the names of the letters?	• Use physical rhythmic movements as the letter name is repeated. March while chanting the letter name. Move arms up and down. Sway from side to side.
Identify the sounds of the letters?	• Use chants that repeat the sound several times, ending with a word that begins with the sound: Example: /e/ /e/ /e/ **egg.**
Produce the sounds of the letters?	• Use mirrors to show the movement of mouth, tongue, teeth as the sound is produced.
Recognize the beginning sounds?	• Use Elkonin boxes – student moves a token into the first box as the beginning sound of the word is said.
Write the letters?	• Write the letter; have students trace it. Create the letter with clay.
Know the names of the pictures?	• Tell students the name of the picture, have students repeat it aloud.
Read high-frequency words?	• Create take-home word cards. Use a reward system to track words learned over time. The student uses the word in a sentence, and the teacher writes it down and highlights the high-frequency word. The student re-reads it the next day.

Identify and Name Medial Short Vowel a RF.K.3b, RF.K.3c

CCSS: RF.K.3
Know and apply grade-level phonics and word analysis skills in decoding words both in isolation and in text.
b. Associate the long and short sounds with common spellings (graphemes) for the five major vowels.
c. Read common high-frequency words by sight.

Lesson Objectives

- Identify and name the letter **Aa.**
- Produce the sound of letter **Aa.**
- Relate the sound /**a**/ to the letter **Aa.**
- Recognize **medial short vowel** sound /**a**/ in words/pictures.
- Read common high-frequency words: **I, like.**

Metacognitive Strategy
- Selective Auditory Attention
- Imagery
- Auditory Representation

Academic Language
- letter name, letter sound, initial sound, medial sound, middle

Additional Materials
- Sound Spelling Card **Aa**
- Blackline Masters 67, 68

Pre-Assess
Student's ability to recognize the sound represented by the target letter of the alphabet and to identify the letter used to represent the corresponding sound.

Introduce

As students participate in this lesson, they will identify the name and sound of the target letter and will identify the letter when the sound and name is given orally. Students will apply their knowledge by recognizing the short sound of the target letter using pictures. Students apply the skill in context by reading simple decodable sentences that include high-frequency words.

State Learning Goal

Say: *The letter **a** is a vowel. It has two sounds. The long sound /ā/ and the short sound /a/. Today we will listen to the short vowel sound of the letter **a** in the middle of words.*

Teach

Say: *Letters represent sounds. We remember the sounds each letter makes. We use letters to write words we say. We use letters to read and write words.*

Phonemic Awareness

Show the picture of the sound/spelling card to review the short sound of /**a**/.

Say: *Listen to this sound: /**a**/. Say it with me: /**aaaa**/. Say it on your own: /**aaaa**/.*

Sound-Spelling Correspondence

Show the letter.

Say: *The way we write the sound /**a**/ is with the letter **a**. The letter **a** makes the sound /**a**/.*

Ask: *What is the name of the letter? (**a**) What is the short sound the letter **a** makes? /**a**/.*

Model

Use BLM 67, Row 1.

Say: *Look at each picture. Say its name. Listen for the short sound of /**a**/ in the middle.*

Ask: *What does the first picture show? Do you hear the sound /**a**/ in the **middle** of the word **bag**?*

Say: *If we hear the sound of **a** in the middle of the word, we will circle the picture. If we do not hear the sound /**a**/ in the middle, we will cross out the picture.*

Practice

Use BLM 67, Row 2.

Say: *Look at the picture. Say its name. Write the letter.*

Ask: *What does the second picture show? (**cat**) Do you hear the sound /**a**/ at the **middle** of the word **cat**? Write the letter **a**. Repeat with other words.*

Apply

Blend Words
Use BLM 67, Row 3

Say: *Look at each letter and listen to the sound as I read.* /**f**/ /**a**/ /**n**/. *Your turn:* /f/ /a/ /n/.

Say: *Now we are going to blend the sounds together by stretching them out as we read them.* Point to each letter in a sweeping motion left to right /**fffaaannn**/.

Ask: *What is the word?* (**fan**) Repeat with other words.

High-Frequency words
Use BLM 67, Row 4.

Say: *First, I will point to the word and read it. Then, you will point to the word and we will read it together. Next, I will read a word and you will point to it. Now, you will read the word and I will point to it. Let's write/trace the word as we spell it:* **like.**

Decodable Text
Use BLM 68, Row 1.

Say: *First, I will point to each word as I read the sentence. Then, you will point to each word and we will read together. Next, I will read the sentence and you will point to each word as I read. Now, you will point to each word as you read. Circle all the* **a** *letters you can find in these sentences. Circle the words* **I** *and* **like** *in the sentences.*

Spelling
Use BLM 68, Row 2.

Say: *Now we can practice writing the sounds we hear in each word. Say one word at a time, stretching each sound. Write a letter for each sound you hear.*

Conclusion

Ask: *What did we learn today? What pictures/words will help you remember the sound* /**a**/ *and the letter* **a**?

Say: *We learned that the letter* **a** *makes the sound* /**a**/ *in the middle of some words.*

Home Connection
Encourage students to practice identifying the medial short vowel sound and writing the letter **a** with a family member. Encourage students to identify other words that have a medial short **a** vowel sound with their family.

✔ Formative Assessment

If the student completes each task correctly, proceed to the next skill in the sequence. If not, refer to suggested intervention 2.

Did the student…?	Intervention 2
Identify the names of the letters?	• Use physical rhythmic movements as the letter name is repeated. March while chanting the letter name. Move arms up and down. Sway from side to side.
Identify the sounds of the letters?	• Repeat the sound several times ending with a word that has the sound. Example: /a/ /a/ /a/ **bat.**
Produce the sounds of the letters?	• Use mirrors to show the movement of mouth, tongue, teeth as the sound is produced. Use hand over mouth to explore movement of air as the sound is produced.
Recognize the beginning sounds?	• Use Elkonin boxes – student moves a token into the first box as the beginning sound of the word is said.
Write the letters?	• Write the letter; have students trace it. Create the letter with clay.
Know the names of the pictures?	• Tell students the name of the picture, have students repeat it aloud.
Read high-frequency words?	• Create take-home word cards. Use a reward system to track words learned over time. The student uses the word in a sentence, and the teacher writes it down and highlights the high-frequency word. The student re-reads it the next day.

Identify and Name Medial Short Vowel i RF.K.3b, RF.K.3c

CCSS: RF.K.3
Know and apply grade-level phonics and word analysis skills in decoding words both in isolation and in text.
b. Associate the long and short sounds with common spellings (graphemes) for the five major vowels.
c. Read common high-frequency words by sight.

Lesson Objectives

- Identify and name the letter **Ii.**
- Produce the sound of letter **Ii**
- Relate the sound /**i**/ to the letter **Ii.**
- Recognize **medial short vowel** sound /**i**/ in words/pictures.
- Read common high-frequency words: **she, can.**

Metacognitive Strategy
- Selective Auditory Attention
- Imagery
- Auditory Representation

Academic Language
- letter name, letter sound, initial sound, medial sound, middle

Additional Materials
- Sound Spelling Card **Ii**
- Blackline Masters 69, 70

Pre-Assess
Student's ability to recognize the sound represented by the target letter of the alphabet and to identify the letter used to represent the corresponding sound.

Introduce

As students participate in this lesson, they identify the name and sound of the target letter, and identify the letter when the sound and name is given orally. Students will apply their knowledge by recognizing the short sound of the target letter using pictures. Students apply the skill in context by reading simple decodable sentences that include high-frequency words.

State Learning Goal

Say: *The letter* **i** *is a vowel. It has two sounds. The long sound* /ī/ *and the short sound* /i/. *Today we will listen to the short vowel sound of the letter* **i** *in the middle of words.*

Teach

Say: *Letters represent sounds. We remember the sounds each letter makes. We use letters to write words we say. We use letters to read and write words.*

Phonemic Awareness

Show the picture of the sound/spelling card to review the short sound of /i/.

Say: *Listen to this sound:* /i/. *Say it with me:* /iii/. *Say it on your own:* /iii/.

Sound-Spelling Correspondence

Show the letter.

Say: *The way we write the sound* /i/ *is with the letter* **i**. *The letter* **i** *makes the short sound* /i/.

Ask: *What is the name of the letter?* (**i**) *What is the short sound the letter* **i** *makes?* /i/.

Model

Use BLM 69, Row 1.

Say: *Look at each picture. Say its name. Listen for the short sound of* /i/ *in the middle.*

Ask: *What does the first picture show? Do you hear the sound* /i/ *in the* **middle** *of the word* **pin**?

Say: *If we hear the sound* /i/ *in the middle of the word, we will circle the picture. If we do not hear the sound* /i/ *in the middle, we will cross out the picture.*

Practice

Use BLM 69, Row 2.

Say: *Look at the picture. Say its name. Write the letter.*

Ask: *What does the second picture show?* (**pig**) *Do you hear the sound* /i/ *at the* **middle** *of the word* **pig**? *Write the letter* **i**. *Repeat with other words.*

Apply

Blend Words

Use BLM 69, Row 3

Say: *Look at each letter and listen to the sound as I read.* /**w**/ /**i**/ /**g**/. *Your turn:* /**w**/ /**i**/ /**g**/.

Say: *Now we are going to blend the sounds together by stretching them out as we read them.* Point to each letter in a sweeping motion left to right /**wiiig**/.

Ask: *What is the word?* (**wig**). Repeat with other words.

High-Frequency words

Use BLM 69, Row 4.

Say: *First, I will point to the word and read it. Then, you will point to the word and we will read it together. Next, I will read a word and you will point to it. Now, you will read the word and I will point to it. Let's write/trace the word as we spell it:* **she.**

Decodable Text

Use BLM 70, Row 1.

Say: *First, I will point to each word as I read the sentence. Then, you will point to each word and we will read together. Next, I will read the sentence and you will point to each word as I read. Now, you will point to each word as you read. Circle all the* **i** *letters you can find in the sentences. Circle the words* **she** *and* **can** *in the sentences.*

Spelling

Use BLM 70, Row 2.

Say: *Now we can practice writing the sounds we hear in each word. Say one word at a time, stretching each sound. Write a letter for each sound you hear.*

Conclusion

Ask: *What did we learn today? What pictures/words will help you remember the sound* /**i**/ *and the letter* **i**?

Say: *We learned that the letter* **i** *makes the sound* /**i**/ *in the middle of some words.*

Home Connection

Encourage students to practice identifying the medial short vowel sound and writing the letter **i** with a family member. Encourage students to identify other words that have a medial short **i** vowel sound with their family.

✔ Formative Assessment

If the student completes each task correctly, proceed to the next skill in the sequence. If not, refer to suggested intervention 2.

Did the student...?	Intervention 2
Identify the names of the letters?	• Use physical rhythmic movements as the letter name is repeated. March while chanting the letter name. Move arms up and down. Sway from side to side.
Identify the sounds of the letters?	• Use repetition and chants that repeat the sound several times with a word that has the sound. Example: /**i**/ /**i**/ /**i**/ **big**.
Produce the sounds of the letters?	• Use mirrors to show the movement of mouth, tongue, teeth as the sound is produced.
Recognize the beginning sounds?	• Use Elkonin boxes – student moves a token into the first box as the beginning sound of the word is said.
Write the letters?	• Write the letter; have students trace it. Create the letter with clay.
Know the names of the pictures?	• Tell students the name of the picture, have students repeat it aloud.
Read high-frequency words?	• Create take-home word cards. Use a reward system to track words learned over time. The student uses the word in a sentence, and the teacher writes it down and highlights the high-frequency word. The student re-reads it the next day.

Identify and Name Medial Short Vowel o RF.K.3b, RF.K.3c

CCSS: RF.K.3
Know and apply grade-level phonics and word analysis skills in decoding words both in isolation and in text.
b. Associate the long and short sounds with common spellings (graphemes) for the five major vowels.
c. Read common high-frequency words by sight.

Lesson Objectives

- Identify and name the letter **Oo.**
- Produce the sound of letter **Oo.**
- Relate the sound /**o**/ to the letter **Oo**.
- Recognize **medial short vowel** sound /**o**/ in words/pictures.
- Read common high-frequency words: **he, has.**

Metacognitive Strategy
- Selective Auditory Attention
- Imagery
- Auditory Representation

Academic Language
- letter name, letter sound, initial sound, medial sound, middle

Additional Materials
- Sound Spelling Card **Oo**
- Blackline Masters 71, 72

Pre-Assess
Student's ability to recognize the sound represented by the target letter of the alphabet and to identify the letter used to represent the corresponding sound.

Introduce

As students participate in this lesson, they will identify the name and sound of the target letter and will identify the letter when the sound and name is given orally. Students will apply their knowledge by recognizing the short sound of the target letter using pictures. Students apply the skill in context by reading simple decodable sentences that include high-frequency words.

State Learning Goal

Say: *The letter* **o** *is a vowel. It has two sounds. The long sound* /ō/ *and the short sound* /o/. *Today we will listen to the short vowel sound of the letter* **o** *in the* **middle** *of words.*

Teach

Say: *Letters represent sounds. We remember the sounds each letter makes. We use letters to write words we say. We use letters to read and write words.*

Phonemic Awareness

Show the picture of the sound/spelling card to review the short sound of /**o**/.

Say: *Listen to this sound:* /**o**/. *Say it with me:* /**ooo**/. *Say it on your own:* /**ooo**/.

Sound-Spelling Correspondence

Show the letter.

Say: *The way we write the sound* /**o**/ *is with the letter* **o**. *The letter* **o** *makes the short sound* /**o**/.

Ask: *What is the name of the letter?* (**o**) *What is the short sound the letter* **o** *makes?* /**o**/.

Model

Use BLM 71, Row 1.

Say: *Look at each picture. Say its name. Listen for the short sound of* /**o**/ *in the middle.*

Ask: *What does the first picture show? Do you hear the sound* /**o**/ *in the middle of the word* **box**?

Say: *If we hear the sound* /**o**/ *in the middle of the word, we will circle the picture. If we do not hear the sound* /**o**/ *in the middle, we will cross out the picture.*

Practice

Use BLM 71, Row 2.

Say: *Look at the picture. Say its name. Write the letter.*

Ask: *What does the second picture show?* (**top**) *Do you hear the sound* /**o**/ *at the middle of the word* **top**? *Write the letter* **o**. *Repeat with other words.*

Apply

Blend Words
Use BLM 71, Row 3

Say: *Look at each letter and listen to the sound as I read. /f/ /o/ /x/. Your turn: /f/ /o/ /x/.*

Say: *Now we are going to blend the sounds together by stretching them out as we read them.* Point to each letter in a sweeping motion left to right /**fffooox**/.

Ask: *What is the word?* (**fox**). Repeat with other words.

High-Frequency words
Use BLM 71, Row 4.

Say: *First, I will point to the word and read it. Then, you will point to the word and we will read it together. Next, I will read a word and you will point to it. Now, you will read the word and I will point to it. Let's write/trace the word as we spell it:* **has.**

Decodable Text
Use BLM 72, Row 1.

Say: *First, I will point to each word as I read the sentence. Then, you will point to each word and we will read together. Next, I will read the sentence and you will point to each word as I read. Now, you will point to each word as you read. Circle all the* **o** *letters you can find in these sentences. Circle the words* **he** *and* **has** *in the sentences.*

Spelling
Use BLM 72, Row 2.

Say: *Now we can practice writing the sounds we hear in each word. Say one word at a time, stretching each sound. Write a letter for each sound you hear.*

Conclusion

Ask: *What did we learn today? What pictures/words will help you remember the sound /o/ and the letter* **o**?

Say: *We learned that the letter* **o** *makes the sound /o/ in the middle of some words.*

Home Connection
Encourage students to practice identifying the medial short vowel sound and writing the letter **o** with a family member. Encourage students to identify other words that have a medial short **o** vowel sound with their family.

✔ Formative Assessment

If the student completes each task correctly, proceed to the next skill in the sequence. If not, refer to suggested intervention 2.

Did the student…?	Intervention 2
Identify the names of the letters?	• Use physical rhythmic movements as the letter name is repeated. March while chanting the letter name. Move arms up and down. Sway from side to side.
Identify the sounds of the letters?	• Repeat the sound several times when a word has the sound. Example: /o/ /o/ /o/ **box.**
Produce the sounds of the letters?	• Use mirrors to show the movement of mouth, tongue, teeth as the sound is produced.
Recognize the beginning sounds?	• Use Elkonin boxes – student moves a token into the first box as the beginning sound of the word is said.
Write the letters?	• Write the letter; have students trace it. Create the letter with clay.
Know the names of the pictures?	• Tell students the name of the picture, have students repeat it aloud.
Read high-frequency words?	• Create take-home word cards. Use a reward system to track words learned over time. The student uses the word in a sentence, and the teacher writes it down and highlights the high-frequency word. The student re-reads it the next day.

Identify and Name Medial Short Vowel u RF.K.3b, RF.K.3c

CCSS: RF.K.3
Know and apply grade-level phonics and word analysis skills in decoding words both in isolation and in text.
b. Associate the long and short sounds with common spellings (graphemes) for the five major vowels.
c. Read common high-frequency words by sight.

Lesson Objectives

- Identify and name the letter **Uu.**
- Produce the sound of letter **Uu.**
- Relate the sound **/u/** to the letter **Uu.**
- Recognize **medial short vowel** sound **/u/** in words/pictures.
- Read common high-frequency words: **with, big.**

Metacognitive Strategy
- Selective Auditory Attention
- Imagery
- Auditory Representation

Academic Language
- letter name, letter sound, initial sound, medial sound, middle

Additional Materials
- Sound Spelling Card **Uu**
- Blackline Masters 73, 74

Pre-Assess
Student's ability to recognize the sound represented by the target letter of the alphabet and to identify the letter used to represent the corresponding sound.

Introduce

As students participate in this lesson, they will identify the name and sound of the target letter and will identify the letter when the sound and name is given orally. Students will apply their knowledge by recognizing the short sound of the target letter using pictures. Students apply the skill in context by reading simple decodable sentences that include high-frequency words.

State Learning Goal

Say: *The letter* **u** *is a vowel. It has two sounds. The long sound /ū/ and the short sound /u/. Today we will listen to the short vowel sound of the letter* **u** *in the middle of words.*

Teach

Say: *Letters represent sounds. We remember the sounds each letter makes. We use letters to write words we say. We use letters to read and write words.*

Phonemic Awareness

Show the picture of the sound/spelling card to review the short sound of /**u**/.

Say: *Listen to this sound /***u***/. Say it with me: /***uuu***/. Say it on your own: /***uuu***/.*

Sound-Spelling Correspondence

Show the letter.

Say: *The way we write the sound /***u***/ is with the letter* **u**. *The letter* **u** *makes the short sound /***u***/.*

Ask: *What is the name of the letter?* (**u**) *What is the short sound the letter* **u** *makes? /***u***/.*

Model

Use BLM 73, Row 1.

Say: *Look at each picture. Say its name. Listen for the short sound of /***u***/ in the middle.*

Ask: *What does the first picture show? Do you hear the sound /***u***/ in the* **middle** *of the word* **bug***?*

Say: *If we hear the sound /***u***/ in the middle of the word, we will circle the picture. If we do not hear the sound /***u***/ in the middle, we will cross out the picture.*

Practice

Use BLM 73, Row 2.

Say: *Look at the picture. Say its name. Write the letter.*

Ask: *What does the second picture show?* (**cup**) *Do you hear the sound /***u***/ in the* **middle** *of the word* **cup***? Write the letter* **u***. Repeat with other words.*

Apply

Blend Words
Use BLM 73, Row 3.

Say: *Look at each letter and listen to the sound as I read:* /**j**/ /**u**/ /**g**/. *Your turn:* /**j**/ /**u**/ /**g**/.

Say: *Now we are going to blend the sounds together by stretching them out as we read them.* Point to each letter in a sweeping motion left to right /**juuug**/.

Ask: *What is the word?* (**jug**) Repeat with other words.

High-Frequency words
Use BLM 73, Row 4

Say: *First, I will point to the word and read it. Then, you will point to the word and we will read it together. Next, I will read a word and you will point to it. Now, you will read the word and I will point to it. Let's write/trace the word as we spell it:* **big**.

Decodable Text
Use BLM 74, Row 1

Say: *First, I will point to each word as I read the sentence. Then, you will point to each word and we will read together. Next, I will read the sentence and you will point to each word as I read. Now, you will point to each word as you read. Circle all the* **u** *letters you can find in these sentences. Circle the words* **with** *and* **big** *in the sentences.*

Spelling
Use BLM 74, Row 2

Say: *Now we can practice writing the sounds we hear in each word. Say one word at a time, stretching each sound. Write a letter for each sound you hear.*

Conclusion

Ask: *What did we learn today? What pictures/words will help you remember the sound* /**u**/ *and the letter* **u**?

Say: *We learned that the letter* **u** *makes the sound* /**u**/ *in the middle of some words.*

Home Connection
Encourage students to practice identifying the medial short vowel sound and writing the letter **u** with a family member. Encourage students to identify other words that have a medial short **u** vowel sound with their family.

✔ Formative Assessment

If the student completes each task correctly, proceed to the next skill in the sequence. If not, refer to suggested Intervention 2.

Did the student…?	Intervention 2
Identify the names of the letters?	• Use physical rhythmic movements as the letter name is repeated. March while chanting the letter name. Move arms up and down. Sway from side to side.
Identify the sounds of the letters?	• Repeat the sound several times with a word that has the sound. Example: /**u**/ /**u**/ /**u**/ **bug**.
Produce the sounds of the letters?	• Use mirrors to show the movement of mouth, tongue, teeth as the sound is produced. • Use hand over mouth to explore movement of air as the sound is produced.
Recognize the beginning sounds?	• Use Elkonin boxes – student moves a token into the first box as the beginning sound of the word is said.
Write the letters?	• Write the letter; have students trace it. Create the letter with clay. • Discuss the letter features (lines, shape). Trace over the letter with multiple colors.
Know the names of the pictures?	• Tell students the name of the picture, have students repeat it aloud. • Discuss the meaning of the word. Use the word in context.
Read high-frequency words?	• Create take-home word cards. Use a reward system to track words learned over time. The student uses the word in a sentence, and the teacher writes it down and highlights the high-frequency word. The student re-reads it the next day.

Identify and Name Medial Short Vowel e RF.K.3b, RF.K.3c

CCSS: RF.K.3
Know and apply grade-level phonics and word analysis skills in decoding words both in isolation and in text.
b. Associate the long and short sounds with common spellings (graphemes) for the five major vowels.
c. Read common high-frequency words by sight.

Lesson Objectives

- Identify and name the letter **Ee.**
- Produce the sound of letter **Ee.**
- Relate the sound **/e/** to the letter **Ee.**
- Recognize **medial short vowel** sound **/e/** in words/pictures.
- Read common high-frequency words: **for, no.**

Metacognitive Strategy
- Selective Auditory Attention
- Imagery
- Auditory Representation

Academic Language
- letter name, letter sound, initial sound, medial sound, middle

Additional Materials
- Sound Spelling Card **Ee**
- Blackline Masters 75, 76

Pre-Assess
Student's ability to recognize the sound represented by the target letter of the alphabet and to identify the letter used to represent the corresponding sound.

Introduce

As students participate in this lesson, they will identify the name and sound of the target letter and will identify the letter when the sound and name is given orally. Students will apply their knowledge by recognizing the short sound of the target letter using pictures. Students apply the skill in context by reading simple decodable sentences that include high-frequency words.

State Learning Goal
Say: *The letter **e** is a vowel. It has two sounds. The long sound /ē/ and the short sound /e/. Today we will listen to the short vowel sound of the letter **e** in the middle of words.*

Teach
Say: *Letters represent sounds. We remember the sounds each letter makes. We use letters to write words we say. We use letters to read and write words.*

Phonemic Awareness
Show the picture of the sound/spelling card to review the short sound of **e**.

Say: *Listen to this sound /e/. Say it with me: /**eee**/. Say it on your own: /**eee**/.*

Sound-Spelling Correspondence
Show the letter.

Say: *The way we write the sound /e/ is with the letter **e**. The letter **e** makes the short sound /e/.*

Ask: *What is the name of the letter?* (**e**) *What is the short sound the letter **e** makes?* /e/.

Model
Use BLM 75, Row 1.

Say: *Look at each picture. Say its name. Listen for the short sound of /e/ in the middle.*

Ask: *What does the first picture show? Do you hear the sound /e/ in the middle of the word **bed**?*

Say: *If we hear the sound /e/ in the middle of the word, we will circle the picture. If we do not hear the sound /e/ in the middle, we will cross out the picture.*

Practice
Use BLM 75, Row 2.

Say: *Look at the picture. Say its name. Write the letter.*

Ask: *What does the second picture show?* (**gem**) *Do you hear the sound /e/ in the middle of the word **gem**? Write the letter **e**. Repeat with other words.*

Apply

Blend Words
Use BLM 75, Row 3.

Say: *Look at each letter and listen to the sound as I read. /**p**/ /**e**/ /**n**/. Your turn: /**p**/ /**e**/ /**n**/.*

Say: *Now we are going to blend the sounds together by stretching them out as we read them.* Point to each letter in a sweeping motion left to right /**peeennn**/.

Ask: *What is the word?* (**pen**) Repeat with other words.

High-Frequency words
Use BLM 75, Row 4

Say: *First, I will point to the word and read it. Then, you will point to the word and we will read it together. Next, I will read a word and you will point to it. Now, you will read the word and I will point to it. Let's write/trace the word as we spell it:* **for.**

Decodable Text
Use BLM 76, Row 1

Say: *First, I will point to each word as I read the sentence. Then, you will point to each word and we will read together. Next, I will read the sentence and you will point to each word as I read. Now, you will point to each word as you read. Circle all the **e** letters you can find in these sentences. Circle the words **for** and **no** in the sentences.*

Spelling
Use BLM 76, Row 2

Say: *Now we can practice writing the sounds we hear in each word. Say one word at a time, stretching each sound. Write a letter for each sound you hear.*

Conclusion

Ask: *What did we learn today? What pictures/words will help you remember the sound /**e**/ and the letter **e**?*

Say: *We learned that the letter e makes the sound /**e**/ in the middle of some words.*

Home Connection
Encourage students to practice identifying the medial short vowel sound and writing the letter **e** with a family member. Encourage students to identify other words that have a medial short **e** vowel sound with their family.

✔ **Formative Assessment**

If the student completes each task correctly, proceed to the next skill in the sequence. If not, refer to suggested Intervention 2.

Did the student…?	Intervention 2
Identify the names of the letters?	• Use physical rhythmic movements as the letter name is repeated. March while chanting the letter name. Move arms up and down. Sway from side to side.
Identify the sounds of the letters?	• Repeat the sound several times with a word that has the sound. Example: /**e**/ /**e**/ /**e**/ **bed.**
Produce the sounds of the letters?	• Use mirrors to show the movement of mouth, tongue, teeth as the sound is produced. • Use hand over mouth to explore movement of air as the sound is produced.
Recognize the beginning sounds?	• Use Elkonin boxes – student moves a token into the first box as the beginning sound of the word is said.
Write the letters?	• Write the letter; have students trace it. Create the letter with clay. • Discuss the letter features (lines, shape). Trace over the letter with multiple colors.
Know the names of the pictures?	• Tell students the name of the picture, have students repeat it aloud. • Discuss the meaning of the word. Use the word in context.
Read high-frequency words?	• Create take-home word cards. Use a reward system to track words learned over time. The student uses the word in a sentence, and the teacher writes it down and highlights the high-frequency word. The student re-reads it the next day.

Recognize CVCe Pattern with Long a RF.K.3b, RF.K.3c

CCSS: RF.K.3
Know and apply grade-level phonics and word analysis skills in decoding words both in isolation and in text.
b. Associate the long sounds with common spellings (graphemes) for the five major vowels.
c. Read common high-frequency words by sight.

Lesson Objectives

- Identify and name the letter **Aa.**
- Produce the sound of letter **Aa.**
- Relate the sound **/a/** to the letter **Aa.**
- Recognize the long vowel sound **/a/** in words/pictures.
- Recognize long vowel sound (CVCe) pattern with long **a.**
- Read common high-frequency words: **of, what.**

Metacognitive Strategy
- Selective Auditory Attention
- Imagery
- Auditory Representation

Academic Language
- letter name, letter sound, vowel, long vowel sound, silent e, pattern

Additional Materials
- Sound Spelling Card **Aa**
- Blackline Masters 77, 78

Pre-Assess
Student's ability to recognize the long vowel sound represented by the target letter of the alphabet and to identify the letter used to represent the corresponding sound.

Student's ability to pronounce the long vowel sound.

Introduce

As students participate in this lesson, they will identify the name and sound of the target letter and will identify the letter when the sound and name is given orally. Students will apply their knowledge by recognizing the sound of the target letter using pictures. Students apply the skill in context by reading decodable simple sentences that include high-frequency words.

State Learning Goal

Say: *Today we will learn to read words with the long sound of the vowel* **a**. *We are going to learn that when we put the vowel* **e** *at the end of some words, the first vowel in the word make its long sound and the vowel* **e** *remains silent.*

Teach

Say: *Letters represent sounds. We remember the sounds each letter makes. We use letters to write words we say. We use letters to read and write words. The letter* **a** *is a vowel. It has a long sound* /ā/ *and a short sound* /**a**/.

Phonemic Awareness

Show the picture of the sound/spelling card to review the long sound of **a**.

Say: *Listen to this sound* /**aaa**/. *Say it with me:* /**aaa**/. *Say it on your own:* /**aaa**/.

Sound-Spelling Correspondence

Write the word **mane** on the board. Point out the vowel **a** in the middle of the word and the vowel **e** at the end.

Say: *When you see the vowel* **e** *at the end of a four-letter word, the* **e** *is silent and the first vowel makes its long sound. Look at the word* **mane**.

Ask: *Does it have the vowel* **e** *at the end?*

Say: *The vowel* **a** *makes its long sound.* Repeat with the words **bake**, **cage**, and **take**.

Model

Use BLM 77, Row 1.

Say: *Look at each picture. Say its name. Listen for the long sound of* **a**.

Ask: *Does it have vowel* **e** *at the end?*

Ask: *Do you hear the long sound of* **a**? *Put a line over the vowel* **a** *and cross out vowel* **e**. *It is silent.*

Practice

Use BLM 77, Row 2.

Say: *Look at each picture. Say its name. Listen for the long sound of* **a**.

Ask: *Does it have the vowel* **e** *at the end? Do you hear the long sound* **a**? *Put a line over the vowel* **a** *and cross out the vowel* **e**. *It is silent.*

Apply

Blend Words

Use BLM 77, Row 3.

Say: *Look at each letter and listen to the long sound of vowel **a** as I read **bake**. Your turn:* **bake**.

Say: *Now we are going to blend the sounds together by stretching them out as we read them.* Point to each letter in a sweeping motion left to right /b̄aaak/.

Ask: *What is the word?* (**bake**) Repeat with other word.

High-Frequency words

Use BLM 77, Row 4

Say: *First, I will point to the word and read it. Then, you will point to the word and we will read it together. Next, I will read a word and you will point to it. Now, you will read the word and I will point to it.*

Decodable Text

Use BLM 78, Row 1

Say: *First, I will point to each word as I read the sentence. Then, you will point to each word and we will read together. Next, I will read the sentence and you will point to each word as I read. Now, you will point to each word as you read. Circle all the **a** letters you can find in these sentences. Circle the words **of** and **what** in the sentences.*

Spelling

Use BLM 78, Row 2

Say: *Now we can practice writing the sounds we hear in each word. Say one word at a time, stretching each sound. Write a letter for each sound you hear.*

Conclusion

Ask: *What did we learn today? What pictures/words will help you remember the long sound of **a** with the silent **e** at the end?*

Say: *We learned that the vowel **a** makes the long sound of **a**, when the vowel **e** is at the end.*

Home Connection

Encourage students to practice identifying long vowel sound **a** in CVCe words with a family member.

✔ Formative Assessment

If the student completes each task correctly, proceed to the next skill in the sequence. If not, refer to suggested Intervention 2.

Did the student…?	Intervention 2
Identify the names of the letters?	• Use physical rhythmic movements as the letter name is repeated. March while chanting the letter name. Move arms up and down. Sway from side to side.
Identify the sounds of the letters?	• Repeat the sound several times with a word that has the sound. Example: /a/ /a/ /a/ **cage**.
Produce the sounds of the letters?	• Use mirrors to show the movement of mouth, tongue, teeth as the sound is produced. • Use hand over mouth to explore movement of air as the sound is produced.
Recognize the CVCe pattern?	• Arrange a list of common same vowel CVCe words vertically, pointing out the pattern.
Know the names of the pictures?	• Tell students the name of the picture, have students repeat it aloud. • Discuss the meaning of the word. Use the word in context.
Read high-frequency words?	• Create take-home word cards. Use a reward system to track words learned over time. The student uses the word in a sentence, and the teacher writes it down and highlights the word. The student re-reads it the next day.

Recognize CVCe Pattern with Long o RF.K.3b, RF.K.3c

CCSS: RF.K.3
Know and apply grade-level phonics and word analysis skills in decoding words both in isolation and in text.
b. Associate the long and short sounds with common spellings (graphemes) for the five major vowels.
c. Read common high-frequency words by sight.

Lesson Objectives

- Identify and name the letter **Oo.**
- Produce the sound of letter **Oo.**
- Relate the sound **/o/** to the letter **Oo.**
- Recognize long vowel sound **o** in words/pictures.
- Recognize long vowel sound (CVCe) pattern with long **o.**
- Read common high-frequency words: **look, my, to.**

Metacognitive Strategy
- Selective Auditory Attention
- Imagery
- Auditory Representation

Academic Language
- letter name, letter sound, vowel, long vowel sound, silent e, pattern

Additional Materials
- Sound Spelling Card **Oo**
- Blackline Masters 79, 80

Pre-Assess
Student's ability to recognize the long vowel sound represented by the target letter of the alphabet and to identify the letter used to represent the corresponding sound.

Student's ability to pronounce the long vowel sound.

Introduce

As students participate in this lesson, they will identify the name and sound of the target letter and will identify the letter when the sound and name is given orally. Students will apply their knowledge by recognizing the sound of the target letter using pictures. Students apply the skill in context by reading decodable simple sentences that include high-frequency words.

State Learning Goal

Say: Today we will learn to read words with the long sound of the vowel **o**. We are going to learn that when we put the vowel **e** at the end of some words, the first vowel in the word make its long sound and the vowel **e** remains silent.

Teach

Say: Letters represent sounds. We remember the sounds each letter makes. We use letters to write words we say. We use letters to read and write words. The letter **o** is a vowel. It has a long sound /ō/ and a short sound /o/.

Phonemic Awareness

Show the picture of the sound/spelling card to review the long sound of **o**.

Say: Listen to this sound /**ooo**/. Say it with me: /**ooo**/. Say it on your own: /**ooo**/.

Say: This is the long sound of the vowel **o**. It sounds like it is saying its name: /**ooo**/. Say it again: /**ooo**/.

Sound-Spelling Correspondence

Write the word **woke** on the board. Point out the vowel **o** in the middle of the word and the vowel **e** at the end.

Say: When you see the vowel **e** at the end of a four-letter word, the **e** is silent and the first vowel makes its long sound. Look at the word **woke**.

Ask: Does it have the vowel **e** at the end?

Say: The vowel **o** says its name. Repeat with **tote, dote,** and **home.**

Model

Use BLM 79, Row 1.

Say: Look at each picture. Say its name. Listen for the long sound of /ō/.

Ask: Does it have the vowel **e** at the end? Do you hear the long sound of **o**? Put a line over the vowel **o** and cross out the vowel **e**. It is silent.

Practice

Use BLM 79, Row 2.

Say: *Look at each picture. Say its name. Listen for the long sound of* **o**.

Ask: *Does it have the vowel* **e** *at the end? Do you hear the long sound* **o**? *Put a line over the vowel* **o** *and cross out the vowel* **e**. *It is silent.*

Apply
Blend Words

Use BLM 79, Row 3.

Say: *Look at each letter and listen to the long sound of the vowel* **o** *as I read the word* **tote**. *Your turn:* **tote**.

Say: *Now we are going to blend the sounds together by stretching them out as we read them.* Point to each letter in a sweeping motion left to right /**tooot**/.

Ask: *What is the word?* (**tote**) *Repeat with other word.*

High-Frequency words

Use BLM 79, Row 4

Say: *First, I will point to the word and read it. Then, you will point to the word and we will read it together. Next, I will read a word and you will point to it. Now, you will read the word and I will point to it.*

Decodable Text

Use BLM 80, Row 1

Say: *First, I will point to each word as I read the sentence. Then, you will point to each word and we will read together. Next, I will read the sentence and you will point to each word as I read. Now, you will point to each word as you read. Circle all the letters* **o** *you can find in these sentences. Circle the words* **look**, **my** *and* **to** *in the sentences.*

Spelling

Use BLM 80, Row 2

Say: *Now we can practice writing the sounds we hear in each word. Say one word at a time, stretching each sound. Write a letter for each sound you hear.*

Conclusion

Ask: *What did we learn today? What pictures/words will help you remember the long sound* /**o**/ *with the silent* **e** *at the end?*

Say: *We learned that the vowel* **o** *makes the long sound* /**ooo**/, *when the vowel* **e** *is at the end.*

Home Connection

Encourage students to practice identifying long vowel sound **o** in CVCe words with a family member.

✔ Formative Assessment

If the student completes each task correctly, proceed to the next skill in the sequence. If not, refer to suggested Intervention 2.

Did the student…?	Intervention 2
Identify the names of the letters?	• Use physical rhythmic movements as the letter name is repeated. March while chanting the letter name. Move arms up and down. Sway from side to side.
Identify the sounds of the letters?	• Repeat the sound several times with a word that has the sound. Example: /o/ /o/ /o/ note.
Produce the sounds of the letters?	• Use mirrors to show the movement of mouth, tongue, teeth as the sound is produced. • Use hand over mouth to explore movement of air as the sound is produced.
Recognize the CVCe pattern?	• Arrange a list of common same vowel CVCe words vertically, pointing out the pattern.
Know the names of the pictures?	• Tell students the name of the picture, have students repeat it aloud. • Discuss the meaning of the word. Use the word in context.
Read high-frequency words?	• Create take-home word cards. Use a reward system to track words learned over time. The student uses the word in a sentence, and the teacher writes it down and highlights the word. The student re-reads it the next day.

Recognize CVCe Pattern with Long i RF.K.3b, RF.K.3c

CCSS: RF.K.3
Know and apply grade-level phonics and word analysis skills in decoding words both in isolation and in text.
b. Associate the long and short sounds with common spellings (graphemes) for the five major vowels.
c. Read common high-frequency words by sight.

Lesson Objectives

- Identify and name the letter **Ii.**
- Produce the sound of letter **Ii.**
- Relate the sound **/i/** to the letter **Ii.**
- Recognize long vowel sound **i** in words/pictures.
- Recognize long vowel sound (CVCe) pattern with long **i.**
- Read common high-frequency words: **put, want.**

Metacognitive Strategy
- Selective Auditory Attention
- Imagery
- Auditory Representation

Academic Language
- letter name, letter sound, vowel, long vowel sound, silent e, pattern

Additional Materials
- Sound Spelling Card **Ii**
- Blackline Masters 81, 82

Pre-Assess
Student's ability to recognize the long vowel sound represented by the target letter of the alphabet and to identify the letter used to represent the corresponding sound.

Student's ability to pronounce the long vowel sound.

Introduce

As students participate in this lesson, they will identify the name and sound of the target letter and will identify the letter when the sound and name is given orally. Students will apply their knowledge by recognizing the sound of the target letter using pictures. Students apply the skill in context by reading decodable simple sentences that include high-frequency words.

State Learning Goal

Say: Today we will learn to read words with the long sound of vowel **i**. We are going to learn that when we put the vowel **e** at the end of some words, the first vowel in the word make its long sound and the vowel **e** remains silent.

Teach

Say: Letters represent sounds. We remember the sounds each letter makes. We use letters to write words we say. We use letters to read and write words. The letter **i** is a vowel. It has a long sound /ī/ and a short sound /i/.

Phonemic Awareness

Show the picture of the sound/spelling card to review the long sound of **i**.

Say: Listen to this sound /īīī/. Say it with me:/īīī/. Say it on your own: /īīī/.

Say: This is the long sound of the vowel /ī/. It sounds like it is saying its name: /īīī/. Say it again: /īīī/.

Sound-Spelling Correspondence

Write the word **like** on the board. Point out the vowel **i** in the middle of the word and the vowel **e** at the end.

Say: When you see the vowel **e** at the end of a four-letter word, the **e** is silent and the first vowel makes its long sound. Look at the word **like**.

Ask: Does it have a vowel **e** at the end?

Say: Vowel **i** is a long **i**. Read it with me: **like**. Repeat with **pike, bite,** and **dime.**

Model

Use BLM 81, Row 1.

Say: Look at each picture. Say its name. Listen for the long sound of **i**.

Ask: Does it have the vowel **e** at the end? Do you hear the long sound of **i**? Put a line over vowel **i** and cross out vowel **e**. It is silent.

Practice

Use BLM 81, Row 2.

Say: *Look at each picture. Say its name. Listen for the long sound of* **i**.

Ask: *Does it have the vowel* **e** *at the end? Do you hear the long* **i** *sound? Put a line over vowel* **i** *and cross out vowel* **e**. *It is silent.*

Apply

Blend Words

Use BLM 81, Row 3.

Say: *Look at each letter and listen to the long sound of vowel* **i** *as I read the word* **bike**. *Your turn:* **bike**.

Say: *Now we are going to blend the sounds together by stretching them out as we read them.* Point to each letter in a sweeping motion left to right /b**i̅i̅i̅**k/.

Ask: *What is the word?* (**bike**) *Repeat with other word.*

High-Frequency words

Use BLM 81, Row 4

Say: *First, I will point to the word and read it. Then, you will point to the word and we will read it together. Next, I will read a word and you will point to it. Now, you will read the word and I will point to it.*

Decodable Text

Use BLM 82, Row 1

Say: *First, I will point to each word as I read the sentence. Then, you will point to each word and we will read together. Next, I will read the sentence and you will point to each word as I read. Now, you will point to each word as you read. Circle all the* **i** *letters you can find in these sentences. Circle the words* **put** *and* **want** *in the sentences.*

Spelling

Use BLM 82, Row 2

Say: *Now we can practice writing the sounds we hear in each word. Say one word at a time, stretching each sound. Write a letter for each sound you hear.*

Conclusion

Ask: *What did we learn today? What pictures/words will help you remember the long sound* /**i**/ *with the silent* **e** *at the end?*

Say: *We learned that the vowel* **i** *makes the long sound* /**i̅i̅i̅**/ *when the vowel* **e** *is at the end.*

Home Connection

Encourage students to practice identifying long vowel sound **i** in CVCe words with a family member.

✔ Formative Assessment

If the student completes each task correctly, proceed to the next skill in the sequence. If not, refer to suggested Intervention 2.

Did the student…?	Intervention 2
Identify the names of the letters?	• Use physical rhythmic movements as the letter name is repeated. March while chanting the letter name. Move arms up and down. Sway from side to side.
Identify the sounds of the letters?	• Repeat the sound several times with a word that has the sound. Example: /i/ /i/ /i/ **bike**.
Produce the sounds of the letters?	• Use mirrors to show the movement of mouth, tongue, teeth as the sound is produced. • Use hand over mouth to explore movement of air as the sound is produced.
Recognize the CVCe pattern?	• Arrange a list of common same vowel CVCe words vertically; point out the pattern.
Know the names of the pictures?	• Tell students the name of the picture, have students repeat it aloud. • Discuss the meaning of the word. Use the word in context.
Read high-frequency words?	• Create take-home word cards. Use a reward system to track words learned over time. The student uses the word in a sentence, and the teacher writes it down and highlights the word. The student re-reads it the next day.

Recognize CVCe Pattern with Long u RF.K.3b, RF.K.3c

CCSS: RF.K.3
Know and apply grade-level phonics and word analysis skills in decoding words both in isolation and in text.
b. Associate the long and short sounds with common spellings (graphemes) for the five major vowels.
c. Read common high-frequency words by sight.

Lesson Objectives

- Identify and name the letter **Uu**.
- Produce the sound of letter **Uu**.
- Relate the sound **/u/** to the letter **Uu**.
- Recognize long vowel sound **u** in words/pictures.
- Recognize long vowel sound (CVCe) pattern with long **u**.
- Read common high-frequency words: **this, saw.**

Metacognitive Strategy
- Selective Auditory Attention
- Imagery
- Auditory Representation

Academic Language
- letter name, letter sound, vowel, long vowel sound, silent e, pattern

Additional Materials
- Sound Spelling Card **Uu**
- Blackline Masters 83, 84

Pre-Assess
Student's ability to recognize the long vowel sound represented by the target letter of the alphabet and to identify the letter used to represent the corresponding sound.

Student's ability to pronounce the long vowel sound.

Introduce

As students participate in this lesson, they will identify the name and sound of the target letter and will identify the letter when the sound and name is given orally. Students will apply their knowledge by recognizing the sound of the target letter using pictures. Students apply the skill in context by reading decodable simple sentences that include high-frequency words.

State Learning Goal

Say: *Today we will learn to read words with the long sound of vowel* **u**. *We are going to learn that when we put the vowel* **e** *at the end of some words, the first vowel in the word make its long sound and the vowel* **e** *remains silent.*

Teach

Say: *Letters represent sounds. We remember the sounds each letter makes. We use letters to write words we say. We use letters to read and write words. The letter* **u** *is a vowel. It has a long sound* /ū/ *and a short sound* /**u**/.

Phonemic Awareness

Show the picture of the sound/spelling card to review the long sound of **u**.

Say: *Listen to this sound* /**ūūū**/. *Say it with me:* /**ūūū**/. *Say it on your own:* /**ūūū**/.

Say: *This is the long sound of vowel* **u**. *It sounds like it is saying its name:* /**ūūū**/. *Say it again:* /**ūūū**/.

Sound-Spelling Correspondence

Write the word **cube** on the board. Point out the vowel **u** in the middle of the word and the vowel **e** at the end.

Say: *When you see vowel* **e** *at the end of a four-letter word, the* **e** *is silent and the first vowel makes its long sound. Look at the word* **cube**.

Ask: *Does it have a vowel* **e** *at the end?*

Say: *Vowel* **u** *is a long* **u**. *Read it with me:* **cube**. *Repeat with* **tube, fuse,** *and* **mule**.

Model

Use BLM 83, Row 1.

Say: *Look at each picture. Say its name. Listen for the long sound of* **u**.

Ask: *Does it have the vowel* **e** *at the end? Do you hear the long sound of* **u**? *Put a line over vowel* **u** *and cross out vowel* **e**. *It is silent.*

Practice

Use BLM 83, Row 2.

Say: *Look at each picture. Say its name. Listen for the long sound of* **u**.

Ask: *Does it have the vowel* **e** *at the end? Do you hear the long sound /***u***/? Put a line over the vowel* **u** *and cross out vowel* **e**. *It is silent.*

Apply

Blend Words

Use BLM 83, Row 3.

Say: *Look at each letter and listen to the long sound of vowel* **u** *as I read the word* **mule**. *Your turn:* **mule**.

Say: *Now we are going to blend the sounds together by stretching them out as we read them.* Point to each letter in a sweeping motion left to right /**mmmuuulll**/.

Ask: *What is the word?* (**mule**) Repeat with other word.

High-Frequency words

Use BLM 83, Row 4

Say: *First, I will point to the word and read it. Then, you will point to the word and we will read it together. Next, I will read a word and you will point to it. Now, you will read the word and I will point to it.*

Decodable Text

Use BLM 84, Row 1

Say: *First, I will point to each word as I read the sentence. Then, you will point to each word and we will read together. Next, I will read the sentence and you will point to each word as I read. Now, you will point to each word as you read. Circle all the* **u** *letters you can find in these sentences. Circle the words* **this** *and* **saw** *in the sentences.*

Spelling

Use BLM 84, Row 2

Say: *Now we can practice writing the sounds we hear in each word. Say one word at a time, stretching each sound. Write a letter for each sound you hear.*

Conclusion

Ask: *What did we learn today? What pictures/words will help you remember the long sound* **u** *with the silent* **e** *at the end?*

Say: *We learned that the vowel* **u** *makes the long sound /***uuu***/, when the vowel* **e** *is at the end.*

Home Connection

Encourage students to practice identifying long vowel sound **u** in CVCe words with a family member.

✔ **Formative Assessment**

If the student completes each task correctly, proceed to the next skill in the sequence. If not, refer to suggested Intervention 2.

Did the student…?	Intervention 2
Identify the names of the letters?	• Use physical rhythmic movements as the letter name is repeated. March while chanting the letter name. Move arms up and down. Sway from side to side.
Identify the sounds of the letters?	• Repeat the sound several times with a word that has the sound. Example: /u/ /u/ /u/ **cube**.
Produce the sounds of the letters?	• Use mirrors to show the movement of mouth, tongue, teeth as the sound is produced. • Use hand over mouth to explore movement of air as the sound is produced.
Recognize the CVCe pattern?	• Arrange a list of common same vowel CVCe words vertically; point out the pattern.
Know the names of the pictures?	• Tell students the name of the picture, have students repeat it aloud. • Discuss the meaning of the word. Use the word in context.
Read high-frequency words?	• Create take-home word cards. Use a reward system to track words learned over time. The student uses the word in a sentence, and the teacher writes it down and highlights the word. The student re-reads it the next day.

Recognize CVCe Pattern with Long e RF.K.3b, RF.K.3c

CCSS: RF.K.3
Know and apply grade-level phonics and word analysis skills in decoding words both in isolation and in text.
b. Associate the long and short sounds with common spellings (graphemes) for the five major vowels.
c. Read common high-frequency words by sight.

Lesson Objectives

- Identify and name the letter **Ee.**
- Produce the sound of letter **Ee.**
- Relate the sound /**e**/ to the letter **Ee.**
- Recognize long vowel sound **e** in words/pictures.
- Recognize long vowel sound (CVCe) pattern with long **e.**
- Read common high-frequency words: **put, this.**

Metacognitive Strategy
- Selective Auditory Attention
- Imagery
- Auditory Representation

Academic Language
- letter name, letter sound, vowel, long vowel sound, silent e, pattern

Additional Materials
- Sound Spelling Card **Ee**
- Blackline Masters 85, 86

Pre-Assess
Student's ability to recognize the long vowel sound represented by the target letter of the alphabet and to identify the letter used to represent the corresponding sound.

Student's ability to pronounce the long vowel sound.

Introduce

As students participate in this lesson, they will identify the name and sound of the target letter and will identify the letter when the sound and name is given orally. Students will apply their knowledge by recognizing the sound of the target letter using pictures. Students apply the skill in context by reading decodable simple sentences that include high-frequency words.

State Learning Goal

Say: *Today we will learn to read words with the long sound of vowel **e**. We are going to learn that when we put the vowel **e** at the end of some words, the first vowel in the word make its long sound and the vowel **e** remains silent.*

Teach

Say: *Letters represent sounds. We remember the sounds each letter makes. We use letters to write words we say. We use letters to read and write words. The letter **e** is a vowel. It has a long sound /ē/ and a short sound /**e**/.*

Phonemic Awareness

Show the picture of the sound/spelling card to review the long sound of **e**.

Say: *Listen to this sound /ēēē/. Say it with me: /ēēē/. Say it on your own: /ēēē/.*

Say: *This is the long sound of vowel **e**. It sounds like it is saying its name: /ēēē/. Say it again: /ēēē/.*

Sound-Spelling Correspondence

Write the word **Gene** on the board. Point out the vowel **e** in the middle of the word and the vowel **e** at the end.

Say: *When you see the vowel **e** at the end of a four-letter word, the **e** is silent and the first vowel makes its long sound. Look at the word **Gene**.*

Ask: *Does it have the vowel **e** at the end?*

Say: *The vowel **e** in the middle of the sentence is a long **e**. Read it with me: **Gene**.* Repeat with **Pete** and **Steve**.

Model

Use BLM 85, Row 1.

Say: *Look at each picture. Say its name. Listen for the long sound of **e**.*

Ask: *Does it have vowel **e** at the end? Do you hear the long sound of **e**? Put a line over vowel e and cross out vowel e at the end of the word. It is silent.*

Practice

Use BLM 83, Row 2.

Say: *Look at each picture. Say its name. Listen for the long sound of* **e**.

Ask: *Does it have the vowel* **e** *at the end? Do you hear the long sound of* **e**? *Put a line over the vowel* **e** *and cross out the second vowel* **e**. *It is silent.*

Apply

Blend Words
Use BLM 85, Row 3.

Say: *Look at each letter and listen to the long sound of the vowel* **e** *as I read the word* **Pete**. *Your turn:* **Pete**.

Say: *Now we are going to blend the sounds together by stretching them out as we read them.* Point to each letter in a sweeping motion left to right /**peeet**/.

Ask: *What is the word?* (**Pete**) Repeat with other word.

High-Frequency words
Use BLM 85, Row 4

Say: *First, I will point to the word and read it. Then, you will point to the word and we will read it together. Next, I will read a word and you will point to it. Now, you will read the word and I will point to it.*

Decodable Text
Use BLM 86, Row 1

Say: *First, I will point to each word as I read the sentence. Then, you will point to each word and we will read together. Next, I will read the sentence and you will point to each word as I read. Now, you will point to each word as you read. Circle all the* **e** *letters you can find in these sentences. Circle the words* **put** *and* **this** *in the sentences.*

Spelling
Use BLM 86, Row 2

Say: *Now we can practice writing the sounds we hear in each word. Say one word at a time, stretching each sound. Write a letter for each sound you hear.*

Conclusion

Ask: *What did we learn today? What pictures/words will help you remember the long sound* **e** *with the silent* **e** *at the end?*

Say: *We learned that the vowel* **e** *makes the long sound* **e**, *when the vowel* **e** *is at the end.*

Home Connection
Encourage students to practice identifying long vowel sound **e** in CVCe words with a family member.

Formative Assessment

If the student completes each task correctly, proceed to the next skill in the sequence. If not, refer to suggested Intervention 2.

Did the student…?	Intervention 2
Identify the names of the letters?	• Use physical rhythmic movements as the letter name is repeated. March while chanting the letter name. Move arms up and down. Sway from side to side.
Identify the sounds of the letters?	• Repeat the sound several times with a word that has the sound. Example: /e/ /e/ /e/ **Pete**.
Produce the sounds of the letters?	• Use mirrors to show the movement of mouth, tongue, teeth as the sound is produced. • Use hand over mouth to explore movement of air as the sound is produced.
Recognize the CVCe pattern?	• Arrange a list of common same vowel CVCe words vertically; point out the pattern.
Know the names of the pictures?	• Tell students the name of the picture, have students repeat it aloud. • Discuss the meaning of the word. Use the word in context.
Read high-frequency words?	• Create take-home word cards. Use a reward system to track words learned over time. The student uses the word in a sentence, and the teacher writes it down and highlights the word. The student re-reads it the next day.

Differentiate Between Long and Short Vowel a RF.K.3b, RF.K.3c

CCSS: RF.K.3
Know and apply grade-level phonics and word analysis skills in decoding words both in isolation and in text.
b. Associate the long and short sounds with common spellings (graphemes) for the five major vowels.
c. Read common high-frequency words by sight.

Lesson Objectives

- Recognize short vowel sounds of **a** in pictures/words.
- Recognize long vowel sound of **a** in pictures/words.
- Differentiate between long and short vowel sounds.
- Read common high-frequency words: **the, is, big.**

Metacognitive Strategy
- Selective Auditory Attention
- Imagery
- Auditory Representation

Academic Language
- letter sound, vowel, long vowel sound

Additional Materials
- Sound Spelling Card **Aa**
- Blackline Masters 87, 88

Pre-Assess
Student's ability to recognize the short vowel sound and long vowel sound represented by each vowel.

Student's ability to distinguish and orally pronounce the short and long vowel sound of each vowel.

Introduce

As students participate in this lesson, they will identify the name and sound of the target letter and will identify the letter when the sound and name is given orally. Students will apply their knowledge by recognizing the sound of the target letter using pictures. Students apply the skill in context by reading decodable simple sentences that include high-frequency words.

State Learning Goal

Say: *Today we will read words with the short vowel sounds and the long vowel sounds of the letter* **a**. *We are going to practice reading short vowel words that have the letter pattern CVC and adding the silent* **e** *at the end to create the letter pattern CVCe so that the first vowel in the word make its long sound and the vowel* **e** *remains silent.*

Teach

Say: *Letters represent sounds. We remember the sounds each letter makes. We use letters to write words we say. We use letters to read and write words. Each vowel has a short sound and a long sound.*

Phonemic Awareness

Show the sound/spelling cards to review the short and long sound of the vowel **a**.

Say: *This is a picture of a* **cat**. *It represents the short sound of vowel* **a**. *Listen to the sound of the short vowel* **a**. *Say it with me:* /**a**/. *Say it on your own:* /**a**/.

Say: *This is a picture of a* **cane**. *It represents the long sound of the vowel* **a**. *This is the long sound of the vowel* **a**. *It sounds like it is saying its name:* /ā/. *Say it again:* /ā/.

Sound-Spelling Correspondence

Write the word **map** on the board. Point out the vowel **a**. Point out the pattern CVC.

Say: *Look at the word* **map**. *Read each sound:* /**m**/ /**a**/ /**p**/. *The vowel says its short sound. What is the word?* (**map**) *Look at the word* **lake**.

Ask: *Does it have the vowel* **e** *at the end?*

Say: *The vowel* **a** *says its name. Read each sound* /**l**/ /**a**/ /**k**/. *The* **e** *at the end is silent. It does not make a sound. What is the word?* (**lake**)

Model

Use BLM 87, Row 1.

Say: *Look at the word* **can**. *The vowel is in the middle.* Read each sound /**c**/ /**a**/ /**n**/. *What is the word?* (**can**) *Look at the word* **game**.

Ask: *Does it have the vowel* **e** *at the end?*

Say: *The vowel* **a** *is a long sound. Read each sound:* /**g**/ /**a**/ /**m**/. *The* **e** *at the end is silent. It does not make a sound. What is the word?* (**game**) Repeat with other words.

Practice

Use BLM 87, Row 2

Say: *Look at the words. Say the words. Listen for the long sound of* **a**.

Ask: *Which words have the vowel* **e** *at the end? Do you hear the long sound of* **a**? Put a line over the vowel **a** and cross out the vowel **e**. It is silent.

Apply

Blend Words

Use BLM 87, Row 3.

Say: *Look at each word. Think: Does it have a silent* **e** *at the end? Will the first vowel say its short sound? Look again: is the vowel in the middle? Will the vowel say its short sound?*

Say: *Now we are going to blend the sounds together by stretching them out as we read them.* Point to each letter in a sweeping motion left to right: /sssaaalll/.

Ask: *What is the word?* (**sale**) Repeat with other words.

High-Frequency words

Use BLM 87, Row 4

Say: *First, I will point to the word and read it. Then, you will point to the word and we will read it together. Next, I will read a word and you will point to it. Now, you will read the word and I will point to it. Let's write/trace the word as we spell it:* **the**.

Decodable Text

Use BLM 88, Row 1

Say: *First, I will point to each word as I read the sentence. Then, you will point to each word and we will read together. Next, I will read the sentence and you will point to each word as I read. Now, you will point to each word as you read. Circle all the long* **a** *and silent* **e** *sounds you can find in these sentences. Circle the words* **the**, **is**, *and* **big** *in the sentences.*

Spelling

Use BLM 88, Row 2

Say: *Now we can practice writing the sounds we hear in each word. Say the word slowly and listen for the short or long vowel* **a**. *Do not forget the silent* **e** *at the end if you hear the vowel say its name.*

Conclusion

Ask: *What did we learn today? What pictures/words will help you remember the long sound of* /**a**/ *with the silent* **e** *at the end? What pictures or words will help you remember the short vowel* **a**?

Say: *We learned that the vowel* **a** *makes a short sound when it is in between two consonants.*

Home Connection

Encourage students to practice identifying short vowel sound of **a** in CVC words and the long sound of **a** in CVCe words with a family member.

✔ Formative Assessment

If the student completes each task correctly, proceed to the next skill in the sequence. If not, refer to suggested Intervention 2.

Did the student…?	Intervention 2
Identify the names of the letters?	• Use physical rhythmic movements as the letter name is repeated. March while chanting the letter name. Move arms up and down. Sway from side to side.
Identify the sounds of the letters?	• Use chants that repeat the sound several times, then a word that includes the sound. Example: /a/ /a/ /a/ **bad** and /ā/ /ā/ /ā/ **bake**.
Produce the sounds of the letters?	• Use mirrors to show the movement of mouth, tongue, teeth as the sound is produced. • Use hand over mouth to explore movement of air as the sound is produced.
Recognize the CVCe pattern?	• Arrange a list of common same vowel CVCe words vertically; point out the pattern.
Know the names of the pictures?	• Tell students the name of the picture, have students repeat it aloud. Discuss the meaning of the word. Use the word in context.
Read high-frequency words?	• Create take-home word cards. Use a reward system to track words learned over time. The student uses the word in a sentence, and the teacher writes it down and highlights the word. The student re-reads it the next day.

Differentiate Between Long and Short Vowel i RF.K.3b, RF.K.3c

CCSS: RF.K.3
Know and apply grade-level phonics and word analysis skills in decoding words both in isolation and in text.
b. Associate the long and short sounds with common spellings (graphemes) for the five major vowels.
c. Read common high-frequency words by sight.

Lesson Objectives

- Recognize short vowel sounds of **i** in pictures/words.
- Recognize long vowel sound of **i** in pictures/words.
- Differentiate between long and short vowel sounds.
- Read common high-frequency words: **I, see, big, like.**

Metacognitive Strategy
- Selective Auditory Attention
- Imagery
- Auditory Representation

Academic Language
- letter sound, vowel, long vowel sound

Additional Materials
- Sound Spelling Card **Ii**
- Blackline Masters 89, 90

Pre-Assess
Student's ability to recognize the short vowel sound and long vowel sound represented by each vowel.

Student's ability to distinguish and orally pronounce the short and long vowel sound of each vowel.

Introduce

As students participate in this lesson, they will identify the name and the long and short sound of sound of the targeted vowel and will identify the letter when the sound and name is given orally. Students will apply their knowledge by distinguishing between long and short vowel sounds in pictures/words. Students apply the skill in context by reading decodable simple sentences that include high-frequency words.

State Learning Goal

Say: *Today we will read words with the short vowel sound and the long vowel sound of the letter i. We are going to practice reading short vowel words that have the letter pattern CVC and adding the silent e at the end to create the letter pattern CVCe so that the first vowel in the word make its long sound and the vowel e remains silent.*

Teach

Say: *Letters represent sounds. We remember the sounds each letter makes. We use letters to write words we say. We use letters to read and write words. Each vowel has a short sound and a long sound.*

Phonemic Awareness

Show the sound/spelling cards to review the short and long sound of the vowel.

Say: *This is a picture of a* **pig**. *It represents the short sound of the vowel* **i**. *Listen to the sound of the short vowel* **i**. *Say it with me: /i/. Say it on your own: /i/.*

Say: *This is a picture of a* **kite**. *It represents the long sound of the vowel* **i**. *This is the long sound of the vowel* **i**. *It sounds like it is saying its name: /ī/. Say it again: /ī/.*

Sound-Spelling Correspondence

Write the word **sit** on the board. Point out the vowel **i**. Point out the pattern CVC.

Say: *Look at the word* **sit**. *Read each sound: /s/ /i/ /t/. The vowel says its short sound. What is the word?* (**sit**) *Look at the word* **bite**.

Ask: *Does it have the vowel* **e** *at the end?*

Say: *Vowel* **i** *says its name.* *Read each sound: /b/ /ī/ /t/. The* **e** *at the end is silent. It does not make a sound. What is the word?* (**bite**)

Model

Use BLM 89, Row 1.

Say: *Look at the word* **hit**. *The vowel is in the middle. It says its short sound.* *Read each sound: /h/ /i/ /t/. Look at the word* **pine**.

Ask: *Does it have the vowel* **e** *at the end?*

Say: *The vowel* **i** *says its name.* *Read each sound: /p/ /ī/ /n/. The* **e** *at the end is silent. It does not make a sound. What is the word?* (**pine**) *Repeat with other words.*

Practice

Use BLM 89, Row 2.

Say: *Look at the word* **fin**. *The vowel is in the middle.* Read each sound: /**f**/ /**i**/ /**n**/. *What is the word?* (**fin**) *Look at the word* **mice**.

Ask: *Does it have the vowel* **e** *at the end?*

Say: *The vowel* **i** *says its name.* Read each sound: /**m**/ /**ī**/ /**s**/. *The* **e** *at the end is silent. It does not make a sound. What is the word?* (**mice**) *Repeat with other words.*

Apply
Blend Words

Use BLM 89, Row 3.

Say: *Look at each word. Think: Does it have a silent* **e** *at the end? Will the first vowel say its name? Look again. Is the vowel in the middle? Will the vowel say its short sound?*

Say: *Now we are going to blend the sounds together by stretching them out as we read them.* Point to each letter in a sweeping motion left to right /**rrrīīīz**/.

Ask: *What is the word?* (**rise**)

High-Frequency words

Use BLM 89, Row 4

Say: *First, I will point to the word and read it. Then, you will point to the word and we will read it together. Next, I will read a word and you will point to it. Now, you will read the word and I will point to it. Let's write/trace the word as we spell it:* **see**.

Decodable Text

Use BLM 90, Row 1

Say: *First, I will point to each word as I read the sentence. Then, you will point to each word and we will read together. Next, I will read the sentence and you will point to each word as I read. Now, you will point to each word as you read. Now, you will point to each word as you read. Circle all the short and long vowel* **i** *letters you can find in these sentences. Circle the words* **I, see, big,** *and* **like** *in the sentences.*

Spelling

Use BLM 90, Row 2

Say: *Let's practice writing the sounds we hear in each word. Say the word slowly. Listen for the short or long vowel* **i**. *Do not forget the silent* **e** *at the end if you hear the vowel say its name.*

Conclusion

Ask: *What did we learn today? What pictures or words will help you remember the short sound of vowel* **i**?

Say: *We learned that the vowel* **i** *makes a short sound when it is in between two consonants. It makes the long sound /ī/ with the silent* **e** *at the end.*

Home Connection

Encourage students to practice identifying short vowel sound of **i** in CVC words and the long sound of **i** in CVCe words with a family member.

✓ Formative Assessment

If the student completes each task correctly, proceed to the next skill in the sequence. If not, refer to suggested Intervention 2.

Did the student…?	Intervention 2
Identify the names of the letters?	• Use physical rhythmic movements as the letter name is repeated. March while chanting the letter name. Move arms up and down. Sway from side to side.
Identify the sounds of the letters?	• Use chants that repeat the sound several times, then a word that includes the sound. Example: /ĭ/ /ĭ/ /ĭ/ **big** and /ĭ/ /ĭ/ /ĭ/ **bike**
Produce the sounds of the letters?	• Use mirrors to show the movement of mouth, tongue, teeth as the sound is produced. • Use hand over mouth to explore movement of air as the sound is produced.
Recognize the CVCe pattern?	• Arrange a list of common same vowel CVCe words vertically; point out the pattern.
Know the names of the pictures?	• Tell students the name of the picture, have students repeat it aloud. Discuss the meaning of the word. Use the word in context.
Read high-frequency words?	• Create take-home word cards. Use a reward system to track words learned over time. The student uses the word in a sentence, and the teacher writes it down and highlights the word. The student re-reads it the next day.

Differentiate Between Long and Short Vowel o RF.K.3b, RF.K.3c

CCSS: RF.K.3
Know and apply grade-level phonics and word analysis skills in decoding words both in isolation and in text.
b. Associate the long and short sounds with common spellings (graphemes) for the five major vowels.
c. Read common high-frequency words by sight

Lesson Objectives

- Recognize short vowel sounds of **o** in pictures/words.
- Recognize long vowel sound of **o** in pictures/words.
- Differentiate between long and short vowel sounds.
- Read common high-frequency words: **We, go, the.**

Metacognitive Strategy
- Selective Auditory Attention
- Imagery
- Auditory Representation

Academic Language
- letter sound, vowel, long vowel sound

Additional Materials
- Sound Spelling Card **Oo**
- Blackline Masters 91, 92

Pre-Assess
Student's ability to recognize the short vowel sound and long vowel sound represented by each vowel.

Student's ability to distinguish and orally pronounce the short and long vowel sound of each vowel.

Introduce

As students participate in this lesson, they will identify the name and the long and short sound of the targeted vowel and will identify the letter when the sound and name is given orally. Students will apply their knowledge by distinguishing between long and short vowel sounds in pictures/words. Students apply the skill in context by reading decodable simple sentences that include high-frequency words.

State Learning Goal

Say: *Today we will read words with the short vowel sound and the long vowel sound of the letter o. We are going to practice reading short vowel words that have the letter pattern CVC and adding the silent e at the end to create the letter pattern CVCe so that the first vowel in the word make its long sound and the vowel e remains silent.*

Teach

Say: *Letters represent sounds. We remember the sounds each letter makes. We use letters to write words we say. We use letters to read and write words. Each vowel has a short sound and a long sound.*

Phonemic Awareness

Show the **o** sound/spelling cards to review the short and long sound of the vowel.

Say: *This is a picture of a **dog**. It represents the short sound of vowel **o**. Listen to the sound of short vowel **o**. Say it with me: /**o**/. Say it on your own: /**o**/.*

Say: *This is a picture of a **cone**. It represents the long sound of vowel **o**. This is the long sound of vowel **o**. It sounds like it is saying its name: /ō/. Say it again: /ō/.*

Sound-Spelling Correspondence

Write the word **not** on the board. Point out the vowel **o**. Point out the pattern CVC.

Say: *Look at the word **not**. Read each sound: /**n**/ /**o**/ /**t**/. The vowel says its short sound. What is the word?* (**not**) *Look at the word **note**.*

Ask: *Does it have the vowel **o** at the end?*

Say: *Vowel **o** says its name. Read each sound: /**n**/ /ō/ /**t**/. The **e** at the end is silent. It does not make a sound. What is the word?* (**note**)

Model

Use BLM 91, Row 1.

Say: *Look at the word **top**. The vowel is in the middle. It says its short sound. Read each sound: /**t**/ /**o**/ /**p**/. Look at the word **hose**.*

Ask: *Does it have the vowel **e** at the end?*

Say: *The vowel **o** says its long sound. Read each sound: /**h**/ /ō/ /**z**/. The **e** at the end is silent. It does not make a sound. What is the word?* (**hose**) *Repeat with other words.*

Practice

Use BLM 91, Row 2.

Say: *Look at the word* **pot**. *The vowel is in the middle.* Read each sound: /**p**/ /**o**/ /**t**/. *What is the word?* (**pot**) *Look at the word* **home**.

Ask: *Does it have the vowel* **e** *at the end?*

Say: *Vowel* **o** *says its name.* Read each sound: /**h**/ /**o**/ /**m**/. *The* **e** *at the end is silent. It does not make a sound. What is the word?* (**home**) Repeat with other words.

Apply

Blend Words

Use BLM 91, Row 3.

Say: *Look at each word. Think: Does it have a silent* **e** *at the end? Will the first vowel say its name? Look again. Is the vowel in the middle? Will the vowel say its short sound?*

Say: *Now we are going to blend the sounds together by stretching them out as we read them.* Point to each letter in a sweeping motion left to right /**rrrooop**/.

Ask: *What is the word?* (**rope**)

High-Frequency words

Use BLM 91, Row 4

Say: *First, I will point to the word and read it. Then, you will point to the word and we will read it together. Next, I will read a word and you will point to it. Now, you will read the word and I will point to it. Let's write/trace the word as we spell it:* **we**.

Decodable Text

Use BLM 92, Row 1

Say: *First, I will point to each word as I read the sentence. Then, you will point to each word and we will read together. Next, I will read the sentence and you will point to each word as I read. Now, you will point to each word as you read. Circle the words* **we**, **go**, *and* **the** *in the sentences.*

Spelling

Use BLM 92, Row 2

Say: *Now we can practice writing the sounds we hear in each word. Say the word slowly. Listen for the short or long vowel* **o**. *Do not forget the silent* **e** *at the end if you hear the vowel say its name.*

Conclusion

Ask: *What did we learn today? What pictures or words will help you remember the short sound of vowel* **o**?

Say: *We learned that the vowel* **o** *makes a short sound when it is in between two consonants. It makes the long sound* /**o**/ *with the silent* **e** *at the end.*

Home Connection

Encourage students to practice identifying short vowel sound of **o** in CVC words and the long sound of **o** in CVCe words with a family member.

✔ Formative Assessment

If the student completes each task correctly, proceed to the next skill in the sequence. If not, refer to suggested Intervention 2.

Did the student…?	Intervention 2
Identify the names of the letters?	• Use physical rhythmic movements as the letter name is repeated. March while chanting the letter name. Move arms up and down. Sway from side to side.
Identify the sounds of the letters?	• Use chants that repeat the sound several times, then a word that includes the sound. Example: /ō/ /ō/ /ō/ **hop** and /ō/ /ō/ /ō/ **hope**
Produce the sounds of the letters?	• Use mirrors to show the movement of mouth, tongue, teeth as the sound is produced. • Use hand over mouth to explore movement of air as the sound is produced.
Recognize the CVCe pattern?	• Arrange a list of common same vowel CVCe words vertically; point out the pattern.
Know the names of the pictures?	• Tell students the name of the picture, have student repeat it aloud. Discuss meaning of the word. Use the word in context.
Read high-frequency words?	• Create take-home word cards. Use a reward system to track words learned over time. The student uses the word in a sentence, and the teacher writes it down and highlights the word. The student re-reads it the next day.

Differentiate Between Long and Short Vowel u RF.K.3b, RF.K.3c

CCSS: RF.K.3
Know and apply grade-level phonics and word analysis skills in decoding words both in isolation and in text.
b. Associate the long and short sounds with common spellings (graphemes) for the five major vowels.
c. Read common high-frequency words by sight

Lesson Objectives

- Recognize short vowel sounds of **u** in pictures/words.
- Recognize long vowel sound of **u** in pictures/words.
- Differentiate between long and short vowel sounds.
- Read common high-frequency words: **I, one, want, is.**

Metacognitive Strategy
- Selective Auditory Attention
- Imagery
- Auditory Representation

Academic Language
- letter sound, vowel, long vowel sound

Additional Materials
- Sound Spelling Card **Uu**
- Blackline Masters 93, 94

Pre-Assess
Student's ability to recognize the short vowel sound and long vowel sound represented by each vowel.

Student's ability to distinguish and orally pronounce the short and long vowel sound of each vowel.

Introduce

As students participate in this lesson, they will identify the name and the long and short sound of the targeted vowel and will identify the letter when the sound and name is given orally. Students will apply their knowledge by distinguishing between long and short vowel sounds in pictures/words. Students apply the skill in context by reading decodable simple sentences that include high-frequency words.

State Learning Goal

Say: *Today we will read words with the short vowel sound and the long vowel sound of the letter* **u***. We are going to practice reading short vowel words that have the letter pattern CVC and adding the silent* **e** *at the end to create the letter pattern CVCe so that the first vowel in the word make its long sound and the vowel* **e** *remains silent.*

Teach

Say: *Letters represent sounds. We remember the sounds each letter makes. We use letters to write words we say. We use letters to read and write words. Each vowel has a short sound and a long sound.*

Phonemic Awareness

Show the sound/spelling cards to review the short and long sound of the vowel.

Say: *This is a picture of a cup. It represents the short sound of vowel* **u***. Listen to the sound of the short vowel* **u***. Say it with me:* /**u**/*. Say it on your own:* /**u**/*.*

Say: *This is a picture of a* **cube***. It represents the long sound of the vowel* **u***. This is the long sound of the vowel* **u***. It sounds like it is saying its name:* /ū/*. Say it again:* /ū/*.*

Sound-Spelling Correspondence

Write the word **bug** on the board. Point out the vowel **u**. Point out the pattern CVC.

Say: *Look at the word* **bug***. Read each sound:* /**b**/ /**u**/ /**g**/*. The vowel says its short sound. What is the word?* (**bug**) *Look at the word* **cute***.*

Ask: *Does it have the vowel* **e** *at the end?*

Say: *The vowel* **u** *says its name.* *Read each sound:* /**k**/ /ū/ /**t**/*. The* **e** *at the end is silent. It does not make a sound. What is the word?* (**cute**)

Model

Use BLM 93, Row 1.

Say: *Look at the word* **cut***. The vowel is in the middle. It says its short sound. Read each sound.* /**k**/ /**u**/ /**t**/*. Look at the word* **rude***.*

Ask: *Does it have the vowel* **e** *at the end?*

Say: *The vowel* **u** *says its name. Read each sound:* /**r**/ /ū/ /**d**/*. The* **e** *at the end is silent. It does not make a sound. What is the word?* (**rude**) *Repeat with other words.*

Practice

Use BLM 93, Row 2.

Say: *Look at the word* **rug**. *The vowel is in the middle.* Read each sound: /**r**/ /**u**/ /**g**/. *What is the word?* (**rug**) *Look at the word* **dune**.

Ask: *Does it have the vowel* **e** *at the end?*

Say: *The vowel* **u** *says its name.* Read each sound: /**d**/ /**ū**/ /**n**/. *The* **e** *at the end is silent. It does not make a sound. What is the word?* (**dune**) *Repeat with other words.*

Apply

Blend Words

Use BLM 93, Row 3.

Say: *Look at each word. Think: Does it have a silent* **e** *at the end? Will the first vowel say its name? Look again. Is the vowel in the middle? Will the vowel say its short sound?*

Say: *Now we are going to blend the sounds together by stretching them out as we read them.* Point to each letter in a sweeping motion left to right /t̄uuunnn/.

Ask: *What is the word?* (**tune**)

High-Frequency words

Use BLM 93, Row 4

Say: *First, I will point to the word and read it. Then, you will point to the word and we will read it together. Next, I will read a word and you will point to it. Now, you will read the word and I will point to it. Let's write/trace the word as we spell it:* **want**.

Decodable Text

Use BLM 94, Row 1

Say: *First, I will point to each word as I read the sentence. Then, you will point to each word and we will read together. Next, I will read the sentence and you will point to each word as I read. Now, you will point to each word as you read.* Circle the high-frequency words **I**, **one**, **want**, *and* **is** *in the sentences.*

Spelling

Use BLM 94, Row 2

Say: *Now we can practice writing the sounds we hear in each word. Call one word at a time, stretching each sound. Say the word slowly. Listen for the short or long vowel* **u**. *Do not forget the silent* **e** *at the end if you hear the vowel say its name.*

Conclusion

Ask: *What did we learn today? What pictures or words will help you remember the short sound of vowel* **u**?

Say: *We learned that the vowel* **u** *makes a short sound when it is in between two consonants. It makes the long sound /**u**/ with the silent* **e** *at the end.*

Home Connection

Encourage students to practice identifying short vowel sound of **u** in CVC words and the long sound of **u** in CVCe words with a family member.

✔ Formative Assessment

If the student completes each task correctly, proceed to the next skill in the sequence. If not, refer to suggested Intervention 2.

Did the student...?	Intervention 2
Identify the names of the letters?	• Use physical rhythmic movements as the letter name is repeated. March while chanting the letter name. Move arms up and down. Sway from side to side.
Identify the sounds of the letters?	• Use chants that repeat the sound several times, then a word that includes the sound. Example: /ū/ /ū/ /ū/ **fun** and /ū/ /ū/ /ū/ **fume**
Produce the sounds of the letters?	• Use mirrors to show the movement of mouth, tongue, teeth as the sound is produced. • Use hand over mouth to explore movement of air as the sound is produced.
Recognize the CVCe pattern?	• Arrange a list of common same vowel CVCe words vertically; point out the pattern.
Know the names of the pictures?	• Tell students the name of the picture, have student repeat it aloud. Discuss the meaning of the word. Use the word in context.
Read high-frequency words?	• Create take-home word cards. Use a reward system to track words learned over time. The student uses the word in a sentence, and the teacher writes it down and highlights the word. The student re-reads it the next day.

Distinguish Sounds Between Similarly Spelled Words RF.K.3b, RF.K.3c, RF.K.3d

CCSS: RF.K.3
Know and apply grade-level phonics and word analysis skills in decoding words both in isolation and in text.
b. Associate the long and short sounds with common spellings (graphemes) for the five major vowels.
c. Read common high-frequency words by sight.
d. Distinguish between similarly spelled words by identifying the sounds of the letters that differ.

Lesson Objectives

- Recognize the difference between two similarly spelled words in pictures/words.
- Distinguish the different meanings of similarly spelled words in pictures/words.
- Use similarly spelled words in context.

Metacognitive Strategy
- Selective Auditory Attention
- Imagery
- Auditory Representation

Academic Language
- letter sound, vowel, sound it out

Additional Materials
- Sound Spelling Cards for short vowel sounds
- Blackline Master 95

Pre-Assess
Student's ability to distinguish between short vowel sounds and consonant sounds represented by letters.

Student's ability to distinguish and orally pronounce the short vowel sounds and consonant sounds of letters.

Introduce

As students participate in this lesson, they will use picture cues to distinguish the spelling between two similarly spelled words. Students will apply their knowledge of short vowel sounds as well as consonants. Students will apply the skills in context by reading simple decodable sentences that include high-frequency words.

State Learning Goal

Say: *Today we will read words that look almost the same. They are spelled with almost the same letters. There may be one letter that is not the same. When one letter in a word changes, the meaning also changes. We will read two words that have similar sound-spellings and we will be able to understand they have different meanings.*

Teach

Say: *Letters represent sounds. We remember the sounds each letter makes. We use letters to write words we say. We use letters to read and write words. When letters change in a word, the meaning of the word also changes.*

Phonemic Awareness

Show the pictures of the sound/spelling cards to review the five short vowel sounds.

Say: *This is a picture of a _____. It represents the short sound of the vowel _____.*

Say: *Listen to the sound of the short vowel /_/. Say it with me: _____. Say it on your own: _____.*

Show picture of sound/spelling cards to review consonant sounds.

Say: *This is a picture of a _____. It represents the short sound of the vowel _____.*
Say: *Listen to the sound of the short vowel /_____/. Say it with me: _____. Say it on your own: _____.*

Sound-Spelling Correspondence

Write the word **big** on the board. Point out the vowel **i**. Point out the CVC pattern.

Say: *Look at the word **big**. Read each sound: /**b**/ /**i**/ /**g**/. The vowel says its short sound. What is the word?* (**big**)

Model

Use BLM 95, Row 1.

Say: *Let's look at the picture of the* **bug**. *What is it? It is a* **bug**.

Say: *Let's look at each of the words. They look almost the same. What is the same?* Point to the letter patterns.

Say: *Do you see that the words are not the same?* Point to the vowel or consonant that differs.

Say: *When a letter in a word changes, the meaning of the word also changes.*

Ask: *Which word do we circle to mean what the picture shows?*

Practice

Use BLM 95, Row 2.

Say: *Look at the picture. What is it? It is a* **dog**.

Say: *Look at each of the words. They look almost the same. What is the same?* Point to the letter patterns.

Ask: *Do you see how the words are not the same?* Point to the vowel or consonant that differs.

Say: *When a letter in a word changes, the meaning of the word also changes.*

Ask: *Which word do we circle to mean what the picture shows?*

Apply

Blend Words

Use BLM 95, Row 3

Say: *Look at the words. Sound them out. Then look at the picture. Write the word that means what the picture shows. Then do the same for the words and pictures in the next row.*

Conclusion

Ask: *What did we learn today?*

Say: *We reviewed short vowel sounds and some consonant sounds. We learned that when a letter in a word changes, the meaning also changes. We read words that looked almost the same, and we chose the word that had the meaning we wanted.*

Home Connection

Encourage students to practice distinguishing between similarly spelled words to confirm their meaning with a family member.

✔ Formative Assessment

If the student completes each task correctly, proceed to the next skill in the sequence. If not, refer to suggested Intervention 2.

Did the student…?	Intervention 2
Identify the names of the letters?	• Use physical rhythmic movements as the letter name is repeated. March while chanting the letter name. Move arms up and down. Sway from side to side.
Produce the sounds of the letters?	• Use mirrors to show the movement of the mouth, tongue, and teeth as the sound is produced. • Use hand over mouth to explore movement of air as the sound is produced.
Recognize letters patterns?	• Arrange a list of CVC words vertically, pointing out the medial vowel in red. Sound out slowly, pointing to each letter, emphasizing short vowel sounds.
Distinguish minimal pairs?	• Arrange minimal pairs of words vertically, pointing out same and different letters. Sound out each slowly, pointing to each letter. Match with pictures. Scramble words and pictures. Have students sound out words and match words to pictures. Do not use nonsense words.
Know the names of pictures?	• Tell students the name of pictures, have student repeat it aloud. Discuss meaning of the word. Use the word in context.
Read high-frequency words?	• Create take-home word cards. Use a reward system to track words learned over time. The student uses the word in a sentence, and the teacher writes it down and highlights the high-frequency word. The student re-reads it the next day.

Read Nouns with Inflectional Endings: -s RF.1.3f

CCSS: RF.1.3f
Know and apply grade-level phonics and word analysis skills in decoding words both in isolation and in text.
f. Read words with inflectional endings.

Lesson Objectives

- Recognize inflectional ending **–s**.
- Recognize singular and plural nouns
- Generalize the meaning of inflectional ending **-s**.

Metacognitive Strategy
- Selective Auditory Attention
- Use Deductive Thinking

Academic Language
- singular, plural, nouns

Additional Materials
- Blackline Master 96

Pre-Assess
Student's ability to recognize ending sound /**s**/ and recognize singular "one" and plural "more than one."

Introduce

As students participate in this lesson, they will understand that singular means "one" and that plural means "more than one." Students will recognize the ending sound /**s**/. Students will generalize the understanding that inflectional ending **–s** changes word meaning from singular to plural.

State Learning Goal

Say: *Today we will show we know that singular means one person, place, animal or thing; and that plural means more than one person, place, animal, or thing.*

Teach

Say: *Nouns are the names of people, places, things, and animals. Singular means "one." Plural means "more than one."*

Ask: *What does singular mean?* Have student echo or repeat: Singular means "one."

Ask: *What does plural mean?* Have student echo or repeat: Plural means "more than one."

Say: *This is the word **cat**. It is a singular noun. It means one cat. Listen to the sound /**s**/. Say the sound /**s**/. I can add **–s** at the end of the word **cat**. Listen to the /**s**/ sound at the end of the word **cats**. It means "more than one cat."*

Model

Use BLM 96, Row 1.

Say: *I look at the first picture. I say its name: **pen**. It is one pen. I look at the next picture. I say its name, **pens**. It is more than one **pen**. I add **–s** at the end of the word **pen**. It is now **pens**. It means "more than one pen."*

Practice

Use BLM 96, Row 2.

Say: *Let's look at the first picture. It is a singular noun. Let's say its name,* **bug**. *It is one* **bug**. *Let's look at the next picture. Let's say its name* **bugs**. *It is more than one* **bug**. *We add* **–s** *at the end of the word* **bug**. *Let's read the word:* **bugs**. *Now it means "more than one bug."*

Apply

Use BLM 96, Rows 3–4.

Say: *Look at the first picture. It is a singular noun. Say its name,* **hat**. *It is one* **hat**. *Look at the next picture. Say its name* **hats**. *It is more than one* **hat**. *Add* **–s** *at the end of the word* **hat**. *Read the word:* **hats**. *Now it means "more than one hat."*

Repeat with **mop**.

Conclusion

Ask: *What did we learn today?*

Say: *We learned that when we add* **–s** *to the end of a singular noun we change it to mean more than one. We can change the meaning of a singular noun to a plural by adding an* **–s**. *Singular means "one." Plural means "more than one."*

Home Connection

Ask students to practice adding **–s** to singular nouns to change them to plural nouns with a family member. Have students identify other words that can be changed from singular to plural by adding **–s** at the end with a family member.

✔ Formative Assessment

If the student completes each task correctly, proceed to the next skill in the sequence. If not, refer to suggested Intervention 2.

Did the student…?	Intervention 2
Pronounce the /s/ in isolation?	• Use mirrors to show the movement of the mouth, tongue, and teeth as the sound is produced. Use hand over mouth to explore movement of air as the sound is produced.
Understand the academic terms *singular* and *plural*?	• Point to the picture showing a singular noun and say: *singular, one ____*. Point to the picture showing the plural noun and say: *plural, more than one, two ____*.
Recognize the names of pictures?	• Say the names of the pictures aloud. Have student repeat the name of the picture. Say: One ____. Then point to the plural and say: *more than one. Two _____*, emphasizing the /s/ at the end of the word.

Decode Words with Common Suffixes: -ful, -ness RF.2.3d

CCSS: RF.2.3d
Know and apply grade-level phonics and word analysis skills in decoding words both in isolation and in text.
d. Decode words with common prefixes and suffixes.

Lesson Objectives

- Recognize and decode common suffixes.
- Recognize that suffixes placed at the end of a root/base word change the meaning of the word.

Metacognitive Strategy
- Selective Auditory Attention
- Use Deductive Thinking
- Generalize a Rule

Academic Language
- word ending, different meaning, suffix, base word, root word
- Note: When using Latin-based suffixes, the base word is called a root word.

Additional Materials
- Blackline Master 97

Pre-Assess
Student's ability to recognize the end of a word as a clue to word meaning

Student's ability to recognize a base or root word as the part of the word that contains meaning and can stand alone

Introduce

As students participate in this lesson, they will understand that suffixes are a group of letters added at the end of a root word to create a new word with a new meaning. Students will recognize and generalize the understanding that suffix -**ful** means "full of, being, having." Students will generalize the understanding that the suffix –**less** means "not having, without."

State Learning Goal

Say: *Today we will practice adding the suffix –**ful** and the suffix –**less** to the end of a word to recognize how they change its meaning. We can use the suffix –**ful** and the suffix –**less** as clues to figure out the meaning of a word.*

Teach

Say: *A suffix is a group of letters that can be added to the end of a word.*

Ask: *To what part of a word is the suffix added? A suffix is added to the end of a word.*

Write the word **color** on the board. Write the suffix –**ful** on the board.

Say: *This is the word **color**. Read it with me: **color**. This is the suffix -**ful**. Read it with me -**ful**. I will add the suffix –**ful** at the end of the word **color** to make the word **colorful**.*

Say: *Read it with me: **colorful**. **Colorful** means "full of color." The meaning of the word **color** changed. For instance, we say, "All of the clowns' colorful costumes." The suffix -**ful** changed the meaning of the word, and created a new word **colorful** that means "full of color."*

Write the word **color** on the board again. Write the suffix –**less** on the board.

Say: *This is the word **color**. Read it with me: **color**. This is the suffix -**less**. Read it with me: –**less**. I will add the suffix –**less** at the end of the word **color** to make the word **colorless**. Read it with me: **colorless**. **Colorless** means "not having color, without color." The meaning of the word **color** changed.*

Say: *When you add a suffix to the end of a word, it changes the meaning of the word.*

Ask: *What happens when you add a suffix to the end of a word? The meaning of the word changes.*

Say: *By adding –**ful** to the word **color**, we created a new word, **colorful**, which means "full of color." By adding –**less** to the word **color**, we created a new word, **colorless**, which means "without color."*

Ask: *What does **colorful** mean? It means "full of color." What does **colorless** mean? It means "without color."*

Model

Use BLM 97, Row 1.

Say: *I read the word* **care**. *I add* **–ful**. *It reads:* **careful**. *It means "full of care." I read the word* **care**. *I add* **–less**. *It reads:* **careless**. *It means "without care." You can use the suffix* **–ful** *and suffix* **–less** *to understand the meaning of a word.*

Practice

Use BLM 97, Rows 2-3

Say: *Let's read the word* **help**. *Let's add* **–ful**. *It reads:* **helpful**. *It means "full of help." Let's read the word* **help**. *Let's add* **–less**. *It reads:* **helpless**. *It means "not having help." You can use the suffix* **–ful** *and suffix* **–less** *to understand the meaning of a word. Repeat with the word* **use.**

Apply

Use BLM 97, Row 4.

Say: *You read the word* **hope**. *You add* **–ful**. *It reads:* **hopeful**.

Ask: *What does it mean?*

Say: *You read the word* **hope**. *You add* **–less**. *It reads:* **hopeless**.

Ask: *What does it mean?*

Say: *You can use the suffix* **–ful** *or suffix* **–less** *to understand the meaning of a word.*

Conclusion

Ask: *What did we learn today?*

Say: *We learned that when we add the suffix* **–ful** *or the suffix* **-less** *to the end of a word, it changes the meaning of the word. The suffix* **–ful** *means "full." The suffix* **-less** *means "not having" or "without."*

Home Connection

Ask students to practice adding -**ful** and –**less** to the end of words and to understand the meaning of the new word created. Have students identify other words that have the suffix –**ful** or –**less** with a family member.

✓ Formative Assessment

If the student completes each task correctly, proceed to the next skill in the sequence. If not, refer to suggested Intervention 2.

Did the student…?	Intervention 2
Recognize and identify the end of a word?	• Point directly to end of the word. Say: *This is the end of the word____ or the last part of the word___.* Then, point to the beginning of the word. Say: *This is the beginning or the first part of the word.*
Understand the meaning of -**ful** and -**less**?	• Show –**ful** and –**less** as opposite categories. Have students sort words under –**ful** and –**less** as the meaning of each pair of opposites are discussed: (**colorful-colorless; joyful-joyless; careful-careless; restful-restless; hopeful-hopeless, flavorful-flavorless**).
Repeat words and phrases when asked?	• Point to the word and have students echo-read, then read it on their own while pointing to the word.

Decode Words with Common Prefixes: re- RF.2.3d

CCSS: RF.2.3d
Know and apply grade-level phonics and word analysis skills in decoding words both in isolation and in text.
d. Decode words with common prefixes and suffixes.

Lesson Objectives

- Recognize and decode common prefixes.
- Recognize that prefixes are placed at the beginning of a root/base word change the meaning of the word.

Metacognitive Strategy
- Selective Auditory Attention
- Use Deductive Thinking
- Generalize a Rule.

Academic Language
- word ending, different meaning, prefix, base word, root word
- Note: When using Latin-based prefixes, the base word is called a root word.

Additional Materials
- Blackline Master 98

Pre-Assess
Student's ability to recognize the beginning of a word as a clue to word meaning.

Student's ability to recognize a base or root word as the part of the word that contains meaning and can stand alone.

Introduce

As students participate in this lesson, they will understand that prefixes are a group of letters added at the beginning of a word to create a new word with a new meaning. Students will recognize and generalize the understanding that the prefix re- means "again, to do again."

State Learning Goal

Say: *Today we will practice adding the prefix **re-** to the beginning of a verb or action word to recognize how it changes its meaning. We will learn we can use the prefix **re-** as a clue to figure out the meaning of a word.*

Teach

Say: *A prefix is a group of letters that can be added to the beginning of a word.*

Ask: *To what part of a word is the prefix added? A prefix is added to the beginning of a word.*

Write the word **do** on the board. Write the prefix **re-** on the board.

Say: *Read it with me: **redo**. Redo means "do again." For instance, we say, We need to redo the work we did yesterday. The prefix **re-** changed the meaning of the word, and created a new word **redo** that means "do again."*

Write the word **count** on the board again. Write the prefix **re-** on the board.

Say: *This is the word **count**. Read it with me: **count**. This is the prefix **re-**. Read it with me: **re-**. I will add the prefix **re-** at the beginning of the word **count** to make the word **recount***

Say: *Read it with me: **recount**. Recount means "count again." For example, we say, "Let's recount the candles on the cake to make sure we have six." The prefix **re-** changed the meaning of the word **count**, and created a new word **recount**, which means "count again."*

Say: *When you add the prefix to the beginning of a word, it creates a new word and changes its meaning.*

Ask: *What happens when you put a prefix at the beginning of a word? The meaning of the word changes.*

Say: *By adding **re-** to a verb or action word, we create a new word, which means "to do the action again."*

Ask: *What does **redo** mean? It means "do again." What does **recount** mean? It means "count again."*

Model

Use BLM 98, Row 1.

Say: *I read the word* **name***. I add* **re-***. It reads:* **rename***. It means "name again." You can use the prefix* **re-** *to understand the meaning of an action word or verb, because the prefix* **re-** *means to "repeat the action" or to "do the action again."* Write the prefix to create the new word.

Practice

Use BLM 98, Rows 2–3.

Say: *Let's read the word* **write***. Let's add* **re-***. It reads:* **rewrite***. It means to "write again." Remember, you can use the prefix* **re-** *to understand the meaning of an action word or verb, because the prefix* **re-** *means to "do again."* Write the prefix to create the new word. Repeat the procedure with **start***.*

Apply

Use BLM 98, Row 4.

Say: *You read the word* **open***. Add* **re-** *at the beginning of the word. It reads:* **reopen***.*

Ask: *What does it mean? It means "open again."*

Say: *You can use the prefix* **re-** *to understand the meaning of an action or verb because the prefix* **re-** *means to "do again."* Write the prefix to create the new word.

Conclusion

Ask: *What did we learn today?*

Say: *We learned that when we add the prefix* **re–** *at the beginning of an action word or verb, it creates a new word that means repeating the action or doing it again.*

Home Connection

Ask students to practice adding **re-** to the beginning of words and to understand the meaning of the new word created. Have students identify action words or verbs to which the prefix **re-** can be added to create a new word with a family member.

✔ Formative Assessment

If the student completes each task correctly, proceed to the next skill in the sequence. If not, refer to suggested Intervention 2.

Did the student…?	Intervention 2
Recognize and identify the beginning of a word?	• Point directly to the beginning of the word. Say: *This is the beginning or the first part of the word ___.* Point directly to the end of the word. Say: *This is the end of the word___ or the last part of the word___.* Say and point: *Show me the beginning of a word. Show me the end of a word.*
Understand the meaning of **re-**?	• Say that to do something again means 'to repeat the action." Then dramatize an action. Say: *I write on a piece of paper. Then I write again.* Say: *I rewrite on a piece of paper.* • Act out: open/reopen, try/retry, name/rename, arrange/rearrange.
Read words?	• Point to each word and have students repeat, echo, then read it on their own while pointing to the word. Use the word in short sentences and explain its meaning to ensure student understanding.

Decode Words with Common Suffixes: -y RF.2.3d

CCSS: RF.2.3d
Know and apply grade-level phonics and word analysis skills in decoding words both in isolation and in text.
d. Decode words with common prefixes and suffixes.

Lesson Objectives

- Recognize and decode common suffixes.
- Recognize that suffixes placed at the end of a root/base word change the meaning of the word.

Metacognitive Strategy
- Selective Auditory Attention
- Use Deductive Thinking
- Generalize a Rule.

Academic Language
- word ending, different meaning, prefix, base word, root word
- Note: When using Latin-based suffixes, the base word is called a root word.

Additional Materials
- Blackline Master 99

Pre-Assess
Student's ability to recognize the end of a word as a clue to word meaning.

Student's ability to recognize a base or root word as the part of the word that contains meaning and can stand alone.

Introduce

As students participate in this lesson, they will understand that suffixes are letters added at the end of a root word to create a new word with a new meaning. Students will recognize and generalize the understanding that suffix –y means "characterized by."

State Learning Goal

Say: *Today we will practice adding the suffix –y to the end of a word to recognize how it changes its meaning. We can use the suffix –y, as a clue to figure out the meaning of a word.*

Teach

Say: *A suffix is a group of letters that can be added to the end of a word.*

Ask: *To what part of a word is the suffix added? A suffix is added to the end of a word.*

Write the word **milk** on the board. Write the suffix **–y** on the board.

Say: *This is the word **milk**. Read it with me: **milk**. This is the suffix **-y**. Read it with me **-y**. I will add the suffix **-y** at the end of the word **milk** to make the word **milky**.*

Say: *Read it with me: **milky**. Milky means "characterized by milk." The meaning of the word milk changed.*

Ask: *What happens when you add a suffix to the end of a word? The meaning of the word changes.*

Say: *By adding **-y** to the word **milk**, we created a new word, **milky**, which means "characterized by milk."*

Ask: *What does **milky** mean? It means "characterized by milk."*

Model

Use BLM 99, Row 1.

Say: *I read the word **silk**. I add **-y**. It reads: **silky**. It means "characterized by silk." You can use the suffix **-y** to understand the meaning of a word.*

Practice

Use BLM 99, Row 2-3.

Say: *Let's read the word* **trick**. *Let's add* **-y**. *It reads:* **tricky**. *It means "characterized by trickiness." Let's read the word* **boss**. *Let's add* **-y**. *It reads:* **bossy**. *It means "characterized by bossiness." You can use the suffix* **-y** *to understand the meaning of a word.*

Apply

Use BLM 99, Row 4.

Say: *You read the word* **curl**. *You add* **-y**. *It reads:* **curly**.

Ask: *What does it mean?*

Say: *You can use the suffix* **-y** *to understand the meaning of a word.*

Conclusion

Ask: *What did we learn today?*

Say: *We learned that when we add the suffix* **–y**, *to the end of a word, it changes the meaning of the word. The suffix* **–y**, *means "characterized by."*

✔ Formative Assessment

If the student completes each task correctly, proceed to the next skill in the sequence. If not, refer to suggested Intervention 2.

Did the student…?	Intervention 2
Recognize and identify the end of a word?	• Point directly to end of the word. Say: *This is the end of the word_____ or the last part of the word_____.* Then, point to the beginning of the word. Say: *This is the beginning or the first part of the word.*
Repeat words and phrases when asked?	• Point to the word and have students echo-read, then read it on their own while pointing to the word.

Name _____ **Date** _____

1.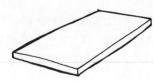

2.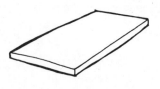

 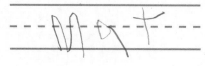

3. **mitt** **mat** **man**

4. [I]

Name _Noah Noa_

Date _____

1. I see the mitt.

I see the mat.

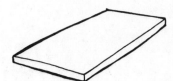

I see the man.

2. Spelling

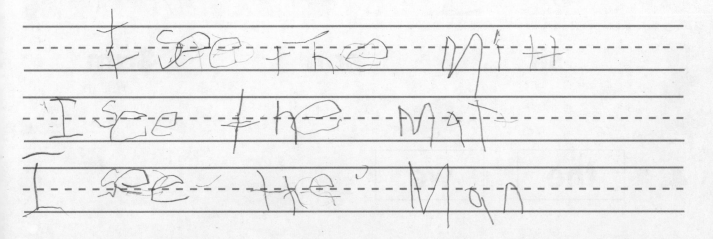

I see the Mitt

I see the Mat

I see the Man

Benchmark Advance · Intervention · Phonics and Word Recognition · Grade K **107**

Name _Noah_ **Date** _____

1.

2.

Sam

Sit _Son_ _Sam_

3.

Sam

sit **son** **Sam**

4. | the | | we |

Name _____   Date _____

1. We sit.

We see the son.

We see Sam.

2. Spelling

We sit

We see the son

We see Sam

Name _____ **Date** _____

1.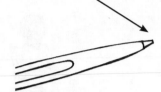

2.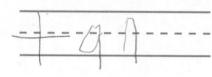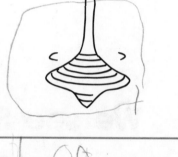

3.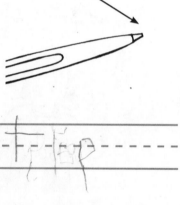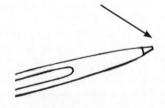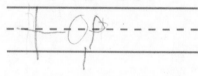

tip   tan   top

4. | see | | go |

Name _____ **Date** _____

1. I see the tip.

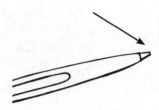

I see her tan.

I will go play with the top.

2. Spelling

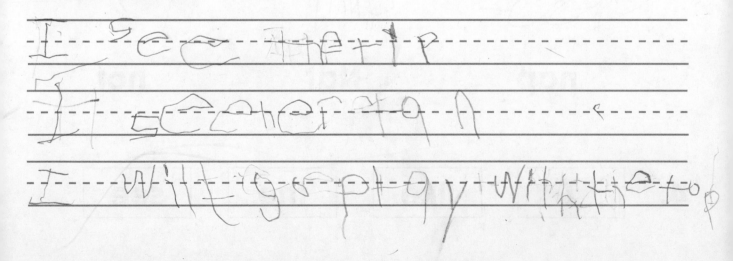

I see the tip

I see her tan

I will go play with the top

Name _____ **Date** _____

1.

2.

nap _Hap_ _Not_

3.

nap   Nat   not

4. | I | | like | | the | | see |

Name _____ **Date** _____

1. I like to nap.

I see Nat.

I see the word not.

2. Spelling

Name _____ **Date** _____

1.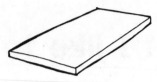

2.

_____ _____ _____
- -
_____ _____ _____

3.

fin   **fan**   **fig**

4. | is | | a |

Name _____   **Date** _____

1. I see a fan.

It is a fin.

It is a fig.

2. Spelling

_____

- -

_____

_____

- -

_____

Name _____   Date _____

1.

2.

_____   _____   _____

- - - - - - - - -   - - - - - - - - -   - - - - - - - - -

_____   _____   _____

3.    

pit   **pin**   **pan**

4. | we | see | is | a |

Name _____ **Date** _____

1. It is a pan.

Is it a pit?

We see a pin.

2. Spelling

_____

- - - - - - - - - - - - - - - - - -

_____

_____

- - - - - - - - - - - - - - - - - -

_____

Name _____ **Date** _____

1.

2.

_____ _____ _____

- - - - - - - - - - - - - - - - - - - - - - - - - - - - - -

_____ _____ _____

3.

car   **cap**   **can**

4. | little | | play |

Name _____ **Date** _____

1. I play in the little car.

I see a can.

He has a little cap.

2. Spelling

Name _____ **Date** _____

1.

2.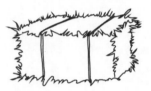

_____ _____ _____

- -

_____ _____ _____

3.

hay   **horse**   **hat**

4. | a | has | he | little |

Name _____ **Date** _____

1. He has a little horse.

We like that hat.

Go see the hay.

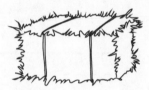

2. Spelling

_____

- -

- -

_____

- -

_____

Name _____   Date _____

1.

2.

‗ ‗ ‗ ‗ ‗   ‗ ‗ ‗ ‗ ‗   ‗ ‗ ‗ ‗ ‗

- - - - -   - - - - -   - - - - -

_____   _____   _____

3.

bib   **bag**   **bat**

4. | and | | you |

Name _____ **Date** _____

1. You see the bag.

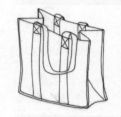

We like the bat.

And he has a bib.

2. Spelling

_____

- -

_____

- -

_____

- -

_____

Name _____ **Date** _____

1.

2.

--- --- ---

3.

rat   **rip**   **run**

4. | he | you | with | big |

Name _____ **Date** _____

1. You see the rat.

The rip is big.

He runs with the girl.

2. Spelling

Name _____ **Date** _____

1.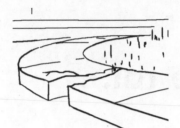

2.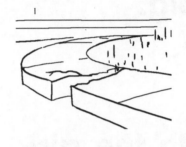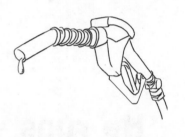

_____ _____ _____
- -
_____ _____ _____

3.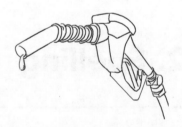

gull   **gap**   **gas**

4. jump   one

Name _____ **Date** _____

1. I see one gull.

She can jump the gap.

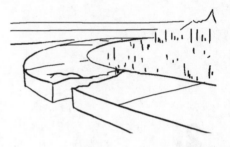

For gas, go one block.

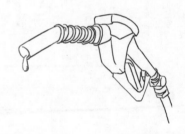

2. Spelling

_____

- -

_____

- -

_____

- -

_____

Name _____ **Date** _____

1.  ●

2.  ●

_____ _____ _____

3.  ●

dog **dot** **dig**

4. | and | you | with | for |

Name _____ **Date** _____

1. I see the dog jump and play.

Look for the big dot.

●

Will you dig with me?

2. Spelling

_____
- - - - - - - - - - - - - - - - - - -
_____
- - - - - - - - - - - - - - - - - - -
_____
- - - - - - - - - - - - - - - - - - -
_____

Name _____ **Date** _____

1.

2.

- -

3.

wig   **wax**   **wed**

4. | **have** | | **are** |

Name _____ **Date** _____

1. I have a wig.

You have a little wax.

The two are wed.

2. Spelling

_____

- -

_____

- -

_____

- -

_____

Name _____ **Date** _____

1.

2.

_____ _____ _____

3.

lid **log** **lap**

4. | said | | two |

Name _____ **Date** _____

1. He said, "Here is the lid."

You two can jump on the log.

She said, "Come sit on my lap."

2. Spelling

Name _____ **Date** _____

1.

2.

_____ _____ _____
- -
_____ _____ _____

3.

jet **jam** **jug**

4. | jump | | have | | one | | for |

Name _____   **Date** _____

1. I jump for the jug.

I have one jar of jam.

I look for a jet.

2. Spelling

_____

- -

_____

- -

_____

- -

_____

Name _____   Date _____

1.

2.

_____   _____   _____
- - - - - - - - - - - - - - -   - - - - - - - - - - - - - - -   - - - - - - - - - - - - - - -
_____   _____   _____

3.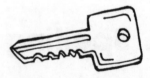

Ken   **kid**   **key**

4. | look | | me |

Name _____ **Date** _____

1. Look at the key.

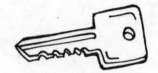

Ken, come to me.

Look at the kid.

2. Spelling

_____

- -

_____

- -

_____

Name _____ **Date** _____

1.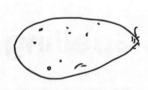

2.

_____

- - - - - - - - - - - - - - - - -

_____

3.

yes   yak   yam

4. | come | | here |

Name _____ **Date** _____

1. Here is a yak.

Yes, it will come.

I like the yam.

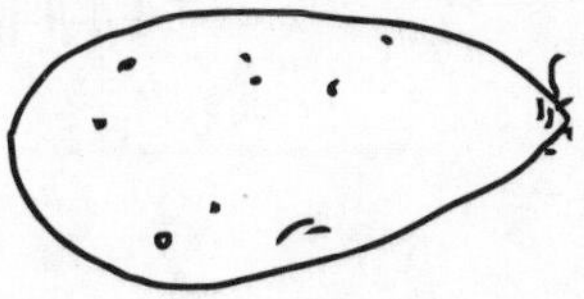

2. Spelling

_____

- -

_____

- -

_____

- -

_____

Name _____ **Date** _____

1.

2.

- -

3.

Val **Vic** **van**

4. | here | look | said | come |

 Benchmark Advance • Intervention • Phonics and Word Recognition • Grade K

Name _____ Date _____

1. The van is here.

Look at Val.

Vic said to come.

2. Spelling

_____

- -

_____

- -

_____

Name _____ **Date** _____

1.

2.

_____ _____ _____

- - - - - - - - - - - - - - - - - - - - - - - - - - - - - - - - - - - -

_____ _____ _____

3.

quit　　　**quiz**　　　**Quin**

4. | **said** | | **come** | | **here** | | **have** |

Name _____ **Date** _____

1. Quin said to come.

Here is the quiz.

We have to quit.

2. Spelling

Name _____ **Date** _____

1.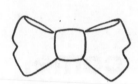

2.

_____ _____ _____

- -

_____ _____ _____

3.

Zak **zip** **zap**

4. | to | | my |

Name _____ Date _____

1. My name is Zak.

I have to zip.

He can jump and zap you.

2. Spelling

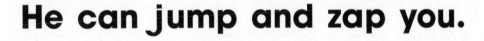

Name _____ **Date** _____

1.

2.

_____ _____ _____

- -

_____ _____ _____

3.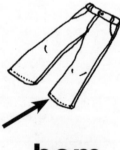

hem   **mom**   **Sam**

4. | **I** |

Name _____   **Date** _____

1. I see mom.

I see Sam.

I see the hem.

2. Spelling

_____
- -
_____
- -
_____
- -
_____

Name _____ **Date** _____

1.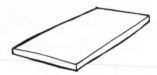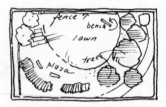

2.

_____ _____ _____
- -
_____ _____ _____

3.

mat   **cat**   **hat**

4. | see | | go |

Name _____ **Date** _____

1. I see the mat.

I go get the hat.

I see the cat.

2. Spelling

_____

- -

_____

- -

_____

Name _____ **Date** _____

1.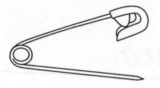

2.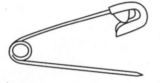

_____ _____ _____

- -

_____ _____ _____

3.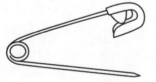

man   **pin**   **can**

4. | like | | the |

Name _____ Date _____

1. I see the man.

I like the pin.

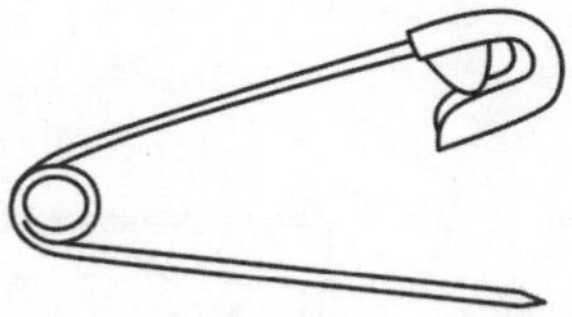

I see the can.

2. Spelling

_____

- -

_____

- -

_____

- -

_____

Name _____ **Date** _____

1.

2.

_____
- - - - - - - - - - - -
_____

3.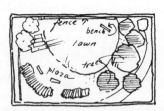

map   **tip**   **sip**

4. | can | | go |

Name _____ **Date** _____

1. Go to the map.

I can see the tip.

I can sip.

2. Spelling

_____

_____

_____

Name _____ **Date** _____

1.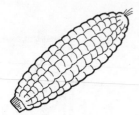

2.

_____   _____   _____
- -
_____   _____   _____

3. 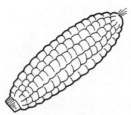   

    cob   **Bob**   **sob**

4. | and | | you |

Name _____ **Date** _____

1. You and I see the cob.

You and I see Bob.

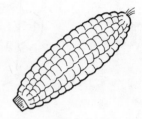

She and I sob.

2. Spelling

_____

- -

_____

- -

_____

Name _____ **Date** _____

1.

2.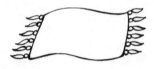

_____ _____ _____
- -
_____ _____ _____

3.

mug   **rug**   **bug**

4. | jump | | one |

Name _____   **Date** _____

1. I see one mug.

I see one rug.

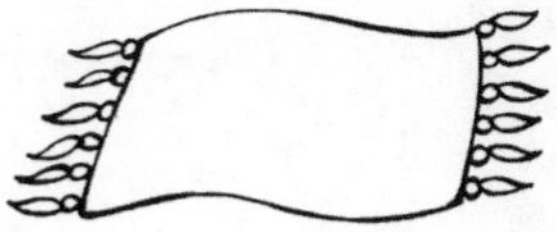

I see the bug jump.

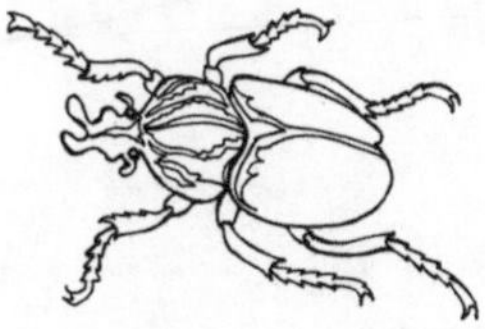

2. Spelling

_____

- -

_____

- -

_____

- -

_____

Name _____ **Date** _____

1.

2.

_____ _____ _____

- -

_____ _____ _____

3.

bed **sad** **kid**

4. | no | | and |

Name _____ **Date** _____

1. No, I am sad.

I am a kid and can jump.

I have a bed and two pillows.

2. Spelling

_____

- -

_____

- -

_____

Name _____ **Date** _____

1.

2.

_____ _____ _____

- -

_____ _____ _____

3.

fox **ox** **Max**

4. | to | | my |

Name _____ **Date** _____

1. I see my fox.

This is my ox.

I like to play with Max.

2. Spelling

_____

- -

_____

- -

_____

- -

_____

Name _____ **Date** _____

1.

2.

_____ _____ _____
- - - - - - - - -   - - - - - - - - -   - - - - - - - - -
_____ _____ _____

3.  

ant   **ax**   **apple**

4. | I | | like |

Name _____ **Date** _____

1. I like the apple.

I like the ant.

I like the ax.

2. Spelling

_____

- -

_____

- -

_____

- -

Name _____ Date _____

1.

2.

_____ _____ _____
- - - - - - - - -   - - - - - - - - -   - - - - - - - - -
_____ _____ _____

3.

ink   **ill**   **in**

4. | **she** | | **can** |

Name _____ **Date** _____

1. She can see ink.

She can go in.

She is ill.

2. Spelling

_____

- -

_____

- -

_____

- -

_____

Name _____ **Date** _____

1.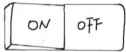

2.       _____

_____

3.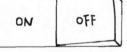

ox   **on**   **off**

4. | he | | has |

Name _____ Date _____

1. He has an ox.

He pushes it on.

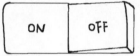

He turns it off.

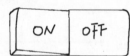

2. Spelling

_____

- -

_____

- -

_____

- -

_____

Name _____ **Date** _____

1.

2.

_____

– – – – – – – – – – – – – – – – –

_____

3.

up   under   umbrella

4. with   big

Name _____ **Date** _____

1. She is up with me.

He is under the big rug.

He has a big umbrella.

2. Spelling

_____
- -
_____
- -
_____
- -
_____

Name _____ **Date** _____

1.

2.   The end

_____ _____ _____

- - - - - - - - - - - - - - - - - - - - - - - - - - - - - - - - -

_____ _____ _____

3.   The end

egg **elf** **end**

4. | **for** | | **no** |

Name _____ Date _____

1. The egg is for him.

No, the elf is small.

This is for the end.

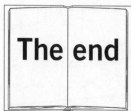

2. Spelling

_____

- -

_____

- -

_____

Name _____ **Date** _____

1.

2.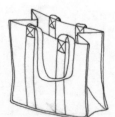

_____ _____ _____
- -
_____ _____ _____

3.

bag   **cat**   **fan**

4. | **I** | | **like** |

Name _____   **Date** _____

1. I like the bag.

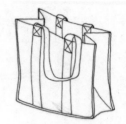

I like the cat.

I see the fan.

2. Spelling

_____

- -

_____

- -

_____

- -

Name _____ **Date** _____

1.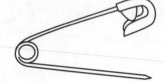

2.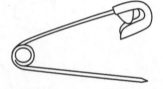

_____ _____ _____
- -
_____ _____ _____

3.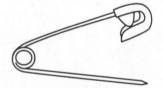

pin   **pig**   **wig**

4. | she | | can |

Name _____ **Date** _____

1. She sees the pin.

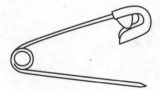

She sees the pig.

I can see the wig.

2. Spelling

- -

- -

Name _____ **Date** _____

1.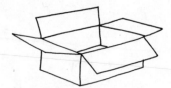

2.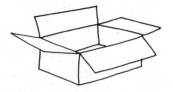

_____ _____ _____
- - - - - - - - - - - - - - - - - - - - - - - - - - - - - - - - - - - - - - - - - - - - - - - -
_____ _____ _____

3.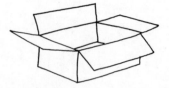

box   **top**   **fox**

4. | he | | has |

Name _____ **Date** _____

1. He has the box.

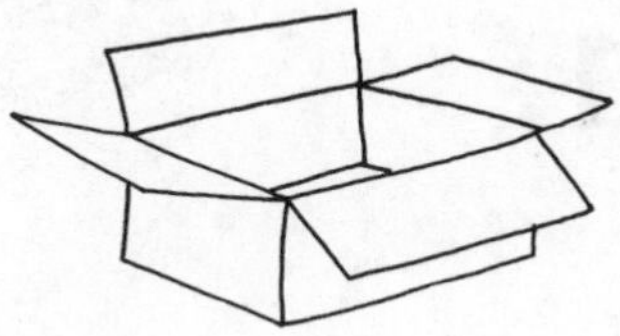

He has the top.

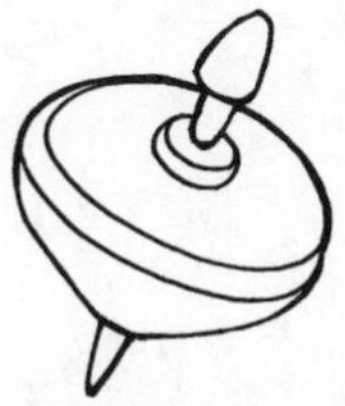

He sees the fox.

2. Spelling

_____

- -

_____

- -

_____

- -

_____

Name _____ **Date** _____

1.

2.

- - - - - - - - - -

3.

bug   **cup**   **jug**

4. | with | | big |

Name _____ **Date** _____

1. I see the big bug.

I like the big cup.

I play with the jug.

2. Spelling

_____

- - - - - - - - - - - - - - - - -

_____

- - - - - - - - - - - - - - - - -

_____

- - - - - - - - - - - - - - - - -

_____

Name _____ **Date** _____

1.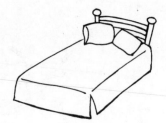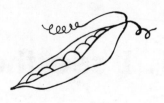

2.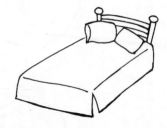

       ———————   ———————   ———————

       – – – – – – –   – – – – – – –   – – – – – – –

       ———————   ———————   ———————

3.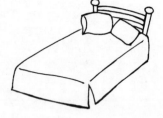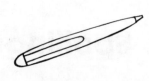

     bed   **gem**   **pen**

4. | for | | no |

Name _____ **Date** _____

1. No, I see the bed.

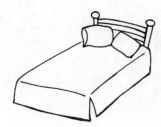

Look for the gem.

No, I see the pen.

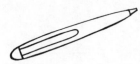

2. Spelling

_____

- -

_____

- -

_____

- -

_____

Name _____ **Date** _____

1.

2.

_____   _____
- - - - - - - - - - - - - - - -   - - - - - - - - - - - - - - - -
_____   _____

3.

cage   **bake**

4. | of | | what |

Name _____ **Date** _____

1. What is in the cage?

What kind of bread did you bake?

2. Spelling

_____

- -

_____

- -

_____

- -

_____

Name _____ Date _____

1.

2.

_____
– – – – – – – – – – – – – – –
_____

3.

woke **tote**

4. | **my** | **to** | **look** |

Name _____ **Date** _____

1. I woke up to the sun.

Look at my tote.

2. Spelling

Name _____   **Date** _____

1.

2.

_____   _____
- - - - - - - - - - - - - - - -   - - - - - - - - - - - - - - - -
_____   _____

3.

dime   **bike**

4. | put | | want |

Name _____ **Date** _____

1. I want the bike.

I put the dime down.

2. Spelling

_____

- -

_____

- -

_____

- -

_____

Name _____   **Date** _____

1.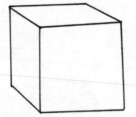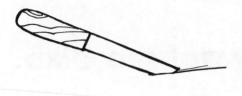

2.

_____   _____

3.

tube   **mule**

4. | this | | saw |

Name _____ **Date** _____

1. I saw the tube.

This is a mule.

2. Spelling

_____

- -

_____

- -

_____

- -

_____

Name _____ **Date** _____

1.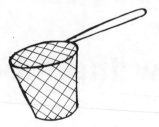

2.

_____ _____
- -
_____ _____

3.

Pete   **Steve**

4. | put | | this |

Name _____ **Date** _____

1. Steve put on his shirt.

This is Pete.

2. Spelling

_____

- -

_____

- -

_____

- -

_____

Name _____ **Date** _____

1.

can **game** **bag** **race**

2.

sat **tale** **bat** **lake**

3.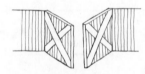

sale **hat** **gate** **pan**

4. | the | is | big |

Name _____   Date _____

1. The hat is big.

The bag is big.

The game is fun.

2. Spelling

_____

- -

_____

- -

_____

Name _____ **Date** _____

 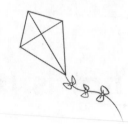

1.

hit   **pine**   **big**   **ride**

2.

fin   **mice**   **lid**   **like**

3.

rise   **pit**   **mine**   **win**

4. | **I** | **see** | **big** | **like** |

Name _____   Date _____

1. I see a big fin.

I like to ride.

I like to win.

2. Spelling

_____
- -
_____

_____
- -
_____

_____
- -
_____

Name _____ **Date** _____

1.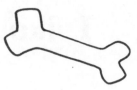

top   hose   hot   bone

2.

pot   home   mom   rose

3.

rope   cow   nose   cap

4 | we | go | the |

Name _____ **Date** _____

1. We go home.

The top spins.

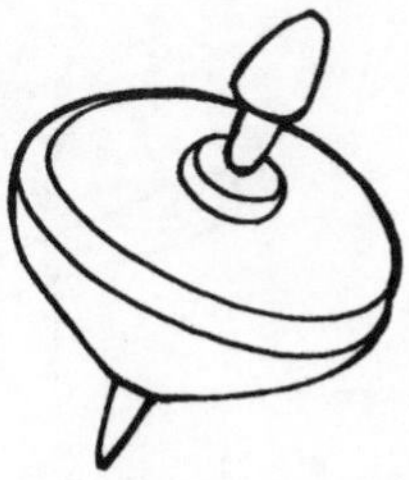

The pot is hot.

2. Spelling

_____

- -

_____

- -

_____

- -

_____

Name _____ Date _____

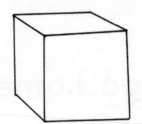

1.

    cut   **rude**   **hut**   **tube**

2.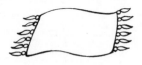

    rug   **dune**   **bun**   **mule**

3.

    tune   **cub**   **huge**   **sun**

4. | **I** | | **want** | | **is** | | **one** |

Name _____ Date _____

1. I want one bun.

The sun is huge.

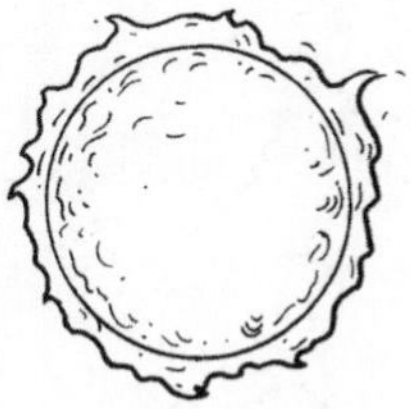

The tube is cut.

2. Spelling

- -

_____

- -

_____

- -

Name _____ Date _____

1.

big

bag

bug

leg

log

led

2.

dog

dig

cat

cut

wig

big

3. My pen is in the [bag] .

My dog likes to [dig] .

I see a big [bug] .

Name _____ **Date** _____

1.

2.

 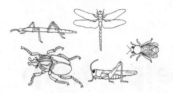

3.

4.

Name _____ Date _____

1. | care | careful | care | careless

2. | help | help____ | help | help____

3. | use | use____ | use | use____

4. | hope | hope____ | hope | hope____

Name _____ Date _____

1. | name | _____ name

2. | write | _____ write

3. | start | _____ start

4. | open | _____ open

Name _____ **Date** _____

1. | silk | silk _____

2. | trick | trick _____

3. | boss | boss _____

4. | curl | curl _____